G000163229

*Supplied by the
international document
delivery service of*

microinfo limited

P.O. BOX 3, NEWMAN LANE,
ALTON, HANTS. GU34 2PG.
ENGLAND
TELEPHONE: 0420-86848
TELEX: 858431 MINFO G

Korea's Competitive Edge

A WORLD BANK RESEARCH PUBLICATION

Korea's Competitive Edge

Managing the Entry
into World Markets

Yung Whee Rhee

Bruce Ross-Larson

Garry Pursell

PUBLISHED FOR THE WORLD BANK
The Johns Hopkins University Press
BALTIMORE AND LONDON

The Johns Hopkins University Press
Baltimore, Maryland 21218, U.S.A.

PRODUCTION   Yamile M. Kahn
BOOK DESIGN   Yamile M. Kahn
FIGURES   Pensri Kimpitak
BINDING DESIGN   Joyce C. Eisen

First printing September 1984

Library of Congress Cataloging in Publication Data

Rhee, Yung W.
  Korea's competitive edge.

  Bibliography: p.
  1. Foreign trade promotion—Korea (South)
  2. Korea (South)—Commerce. I. Ross-Larson, Bruce Clifford, 1942–
  II. Pursell, Garry. III. Title.
  HF1602.5.R47 1984   *382′ .095195*   *84-47956*
  ISBN 0-8018-3266-7

Contents

Introductory Note

THIS STUDY IS BASED ON A SURVEY of 113 Korean exporting firms that Yung Whee Rhee and Garry Pursell conducted in the summer and early fall of 1976. The survey had two parts—one financial, the other descriptive—and was extremely detailed, with the questionnaire running to some 500 pages. The firms in the sample were much larger than average Korean firms: they had average annual sales of $32 million, compared with $0.5 million nationwide, and average work forces of more than 2,500, compared with about fifty nationwide. The research is part of a larger project examining export incentive policies in the developing countries, a project under the general direction of Bela Balassa. Only the results from the descriptive part of the survey are reported here. Those from the financial part will be published later.

Acknowledgments

WITHOUT THE GRACIOUS COOPERATION OF FIRMS and the unflagging support of the Korea Ministry of Commerce and Industry, it would not have been possible to conduct the survey, let alone garner such complete responses. Bela Balassa, Parvez Hasan, Fred Moore, Ram Agarwala, Don Keesing, and an anonymous referee commented on the original manuscript and helped greatly in improving it. Larry Westphal insisted on sharper arguments and clearer interpretations of the findings at each step of the way. Without his guidance and continuing encouragement, this would never have become a book.

Korea's Competitive Edge

1

Introduction

KOREA'S REMARKABLE EXPORT GROWTH is the envy of much of the developing world. The country's exports—worth $52 million in 1962, the year the export drive began—passed $100 million in 1964, $500 million in 1968, $1 billion in 1970, $10 billion in 1977, and $20 billion in 1981. More than 90 percent of the exports in 1981 were manufactured goods, roughly a sixth of the manufactured exports by developing countries. Traditional export products, such as wigs, plywood, footwear, and textiles have led the way. But by the mid-1970s Korean exporters had diversified their array of traditional products and moved into the export of ships, electronics, and iron and steel products. Korean exporters have also been diversifying their markets. In 1974 Japan and the United States took more than 70 percent of Korea's exports. In 1980 that share was down to 44 percent, as Korean exporters broke into new markets in Europe, the Middle East, and the rest of the developing world. The rapid growth of trade—with exports growing almost 25 percent a year in constant prices, imports 17 percent a year—led the growth of the Korean economy at 9 percent a year during most of the 1960s and 1970s.[1]

Why has Korea been so successful in managing its entry into world markets and in acquiring and then maintaining a competitive edge in those markets? Balassa (1976, 1982), Westphal (1978), and several others have promoted the view that Korean incentives have been close enough to being right much of the time to enable Korean producers to exploit the country's comparative advantage in export production. In essence, the officials manipulating the policy tools were able to devise incentives that, on the average, eliminated discrimination against producing for export. Producers suffered no substantial disadvantages by producing for the export market; they could let

3

profit guide their decisions about whether and how much to produce for the export market, whether and how much for the domestic market. Korea was thus able to reap the benefits of an outward-looking development strategy: export growth was dramatic, import substitution was efficient, and import restrictions were gradually lifted.[2]

For the basic incentives, access was automatic for all production and commercial transactions related to exports. But the determination of those incentives and the administration of systems to ensure access to them were not simple tasks for the export bureaucracy. The incentives and the systems ensuring access to them had to be adjusted through continuing evaluation by the government in response to changing circumstances at home and abroad. When the incentives were wrong, the government had to adjust the incentives to make them right. So, without the right process of setting, implementing, and maintaining incentives, Korea could not have had the right incentives. The process thus deserves as much attention as do the incentives.

Westphal (1978) and Mason and his colleagues (1980) have stressed the importance of institutions inherited from the predevelopmental era, the commitment of the political leadership to growth, and the pragmatic approach of the bureaucracy to policy implementation. But as Krueger (1981) writes, the interactions between the choice of policies and the other important economic and political variables are not well understood.

Coupled with the right policies, Korea's heritage of social, political, and economic institutions has been important in the country's industrialization—as has the cultural background of Koreans. Korea in 1960 may have been labeled as an economic basket case incapable of sustained development, but the country was no stranger to industry. When the country shifted gears in the early 1960s, considerable industrial experience accumulated over the preceding five or six decades lay just beneath the surface of the foundation of Korea's industrial takeoff. Nor was the Korean worker lacking the latent talent needed for industriousness on the job. Reasonably well educated and often highly experienced, the Korean worker had another important attribute: adherence to Confucian beliefs, which place a high value on loyalty, punctuality, hard work, and respect for authority. True, the same colonial experience, the same characteristics of Koreans, the same Confucian beliefs could be blamed for inhibiting economic development before the 1960s. But coupled with the right policies, those underlying forces were unleashed to promote rapid development.

Korea's political leadership believed, from the beginning of the export drive in the early 1960s until the middle of the 1970s, that outward-looking policies for trade and industry were essential for the country's development. The government continually affirmed its sustained commitment to exporting as the engine of economic growth. As a result, the policies for export promotion had a permanence that has reassured firms that the rules of the game would not suddenly be reversed. The pragmatic implementation of policy also was instrumental in Korea's success in exporting. With exporting as the prime national objective, few other policies were allowed to conflict with outward-looking economic policies. And with so much attention given to the success of exporting, it was possible to retreat from policies that proved ineffective.

Jones and Sakong (1980) have contributed to the understanding of Korea's economic growth by exploring in detail the relations between business and government. In their view, the institutional framework for economic decision-making is crucial to a country's development—and fundamental to that framework is the relationship between business and government. They stress the organizational and behavioral aspects at the heart of economic decisions, emphasizing the government's dominant role as the most important aspect. They also describe the government's compliance mechanisms that selectively guide the behavior of entrepreneurs and managers.

Many of these studies point to the importance of the institutional setup for economic decision-making, but none of them explores the dynamism and inner workings of that setup. The incentives may have been right, but what administrative arrangements enabled them to be right? The political leadership may have been committed to economic development, but how was that commitment translated into action by the bureaucracy and by firms? The relations between business and government may have been close, but why were they close and what were their underpinnings?

More and more the institutional setup for economic decision-making looms large in explaining why some economies export successfully. Take Japan, Korea, Hong Kong, and Singapore. What appear as common to their success in exporting, in addition to their outward-looking development strategies, are an active private sector, weak labor organizations, and an efficient bureaucracy that has created a climate conducive to the conduct of business. Also common to their success is a set of strong institutional mechanisms that support the alliance of business and government in the effort to export. Those mechanisms naturally differ from economy to economy because they emerge from different backgrounds and in different circumstances. For example: In Korea the government has had control of the banks, whereas banks in Japan have been heavily influenced by the private sector, especially the trading companies. In Korea (as well as Japan and Singapore) the domestic market has been selectively protected, whereas in Hong Kong there has been little protection of the domestic market. And in Korea direct foreign investment has been important in only a few sectors, whereas in Singapore it has been important in many sectors. What bears restating is that each of these economies has developed institutional mechanisms appropriate to its historical background and circumstances—mechanisms that support the alliance of business and government in the effort to export (see Hofheinz and Calder 1982).

Foreign resources have also been a factor in Korea's success in exporting. The mix of foreign and domestic capital, and its role in the rapid growth of the 1960s and 1970s has been analyzed by Frank, Kim, and Westphal (1975) and by Krueger (1980). Korea has relied heavily on flows of foreign capital resources, though these inflows have for the most part been debt, not equity. But less is known about importance of foreign and domestic actors in two other activities that firms must engage in to compete internationally: acquiring and mastering technology, and marketing overseas. The success of Korea on the international marketplace has depended first and foremost on the efficiency of firms in production, a subject adequately analyzed in many earlier studies of Korea. But it has depended, too, on the ways Korean firms acquire and master technology and on the ways that firms market (or let others market) their products overseas—processes that have some of their elements described in Westphal, Rhee, and Pursell (1981). Involving different costs and benefits, the methods firms select for acquiring technology and for marketing overseas clearly impinge on the ability of those firms to export.

Our intention in this book is to broaden the discussion of Korea's competitive edge by developing the two foregoing themes: the first has to do with the intricacies and inner workings of the main institutions for export promotion in Korea; the second with the selectivity possible in acquiring technology and in marketing products overseas. In chapter 2 we describe the system of export incentives in Korea. In chapter 3 we examine the way exporters regard two key institutions of the Korean incentive system—the export targets and monthly trade promotion meetings—and we spell out some of contributions of those institutions to informational efficiency and to the effectiveness of the entire system of export promotion. In chapter 4 we examine the ways of acquiring technology that Korean exporters regard as important for their main products and processes—and what is involved in mastering new technology. In chapter 5 we examine who does what in marketing Korean exports. In chapter 6 we explain the probable causes of Korea's setbacks in the late 1970s, speculate about some of the challenges Korean exporters face in the 1980s, and detail some of the lessons of Korea's experience for other developing countries.

Notes to Chapter 1

1. The Republic of Korea, or South Korea, will generally be referred to in this book as Korea. The numbers in this paragraph are from appendix B, which gives basic economic data on Korea for 1962–81. For the improvements in national welfare associated with Korea's economic growth, see Mason and others (1980).

2. All this is consistent with the conclusions of empirical studies of the effect of foreign trade regimes on the economic growth of developing countries: countries with outward-looking strategies have had better export performance and better economic growth than countries with inward-looking strategies; the trade regimes under outward-looking strategies have been close to free trade regimes for export products (World Bank: Balassa and associates 1971, 1982; Organization for Economic Cooperation and Development: Little, Scitovsky, and Scott 1970; National Bureau of Economic Research: Bhagwati 1978 and Krueger 1978).

2

Export Incentives

MOST DEVELOPING COUNTRIES IMPOSE TARIFFS on imports to raise revenue and to protect the domestic market. Many of these countries also place quantitative restrictions on imports to give additional protection to local industries producing for the domestic market. These policies have three main consequences for would-be exporters. First, the prices that goods can be sold for on the domestic market are higher than those on the world market. Second, the prices that must be paid for imported intermediate inputs are higher than world prices. Third, the balance-of-payments equilibrium can, because of reduced imports, be maintained at an exchange rate more unfavorable to exporters than otherwise. All three consequences reduce the profitability of exporting relative to that of producing for the domestic market. The profitability of exporting is further reduced if the exchange rate is not adjusted when domestic prices rise faster than world prices: the increasingly overvalued exchange rate further reduces the prices producers receive in domestic currency for their exports.

To remove these biases against exporting, a government need only open its borders to free trade and let its currency float to its equilibrium exchange rate. For many developing countries, such liberalization would be desirable as a policy for the medium and long term. But in the short term these actions would allow imports to displace much local production, including that by infant industries being temporarily protected, and increase the deficit in the balance of payments. Nor do the developing countries find it easy to allow their exchange rates to float to the equilibrium level. Their financial markets are not competitive. Their financial institutions are not well developed. Their

9

currencies are not automatically convertible. And their capital flows are not free.[1] So rather than open their borders to free trade, many developing country governments try to establish a free trade regime for exporting side by side with the protected trade regime for production for the domestic market—say, by allowing unrestricted, tariff-free imports of raw materials and intermediate inputs for export production. Rather than allow free flows of capital, they selectively control inflows and outflows. And rather than float their currencies, they adjust them regularly or from time to time. In addition to these adjustments, they can, for example, provide tax, financial, and other incentives to compensate exporters for the overvaluation of the exchange rate.

Another requirement of exporting is readily available credit. Getting bank loans is not a big problem in developed countries, where money and capital markets are well developed. But in most developing countries, those markets are not developed. That can make it difficult for firms to finance export production. Even if financial markets are developing, they typically favor large firms over small. And the procedures for approving loans often are unwieldy, time-consuming, and burdened by requirements for physical collateral that often cannot be met. These difficulties can conspire to put developing-country exporters at a big disadvantage in world markets.

The first requirements in reducing the disincentives to exporting, then, are to guarantee producers free access to imported intermediate inputs and export financing—and to grant additional incentives that compensate them for an overvalued exchange rate. Doing these things is no simple matter, however. Tariffs on imported inputs for export production may be refunded later. But if this takes months or years rather than days or weeks, producers are not going to brave the uncertainty. Bank loans may be available for working capital at preferential rates. But if it takes months for export loans to be approved at the discretion of a bank manager, would-be exporters are not going to be able to meet orders at the speed required on the international marketplace. And certain taxes may be set at lower rates for export production. But if left to the case-by-case discretion of tax officials, would-be exporters once again are not going to brave the uncertainty. What is needed is for the incentives to be automatic and immediate—but making them automatic and immediate is not a simple task. And unless this task is done well, firms and entrepreneurs may be unable or unwilling to respond to incentives a government grants to remove the bias against exporting.

Basic Incentives and Their Administration

In Korea there have been two key systems for administering the basic export incentives: one for granting unrestricted and tariff-free access to the imported intermediate inputs needed in export production; the other for granting automatic access to bank loans for the working capital needed for all export activity. Korea also has not shied away from periodic devaluations—which have ensured that domestic inflation, regularly in excess of world inflation, would not lead to substantial and sustained overvaluation of the real exchange rate for exports. The exporters' costs of temporary overvaluation have been compensated for in part by preferential interest rates. The underlying objective has been to remove the bias against producing for export and to give exporters just the incentives they need to be on an equal footing with producers from other countries in competing in world markets.

The unrestricted, tariff-free access to imported inputs establishes a free trade regime for export activities and allows producers to choose between suppliers at home and abroad when purchasing their intermediate inputs for export production. They can thus buy those inputs at world prices and suffer no disadvantage in the prices they pay for their raw materials. The access to bank loans for working capital for export production is automatic because the central bank will automatically rediscount the export loans that commercial banks make to firms. As was pointed out earlier, would-be exporters can be easily discouraged from producing for export if the access to imported inputs and export loans is discretionary and slow. Producers in Korea are not so discouraged. The guiding principle in creating the free trade regime and in providing export loans for working capital has been to treat all export activity the same way:

- Whether by a fishing company that trawls for tuna, by a highly specialized manufacturing firm that produces precision instruments, or by a construction company putting up power plants in the Middle East.
- Whether by a large conglomerate that exports more than $1 billion a year or by a small firm barely above the threshold of $1 million a year that qualifies it for an exporter's license.
- Whether by a direct exporter (say, a shirt manufacturer), by a supplier of that direct exporter (a maker of cotton cloth), or by a supplier of that supplier (producer of cotton thread).

With the access to tariff-free inputs and export loans automatic, the exchange rate and the preferential interest rates have been adjusted from time to time. But the real fine-tuning of the export incentive system is in the administrative arrangements that govern the day-to-day transactions between firms and the export bureaucracy. As was mentioned earlier, the incentives cannot be right if firms do not have access to them. Efficient administrative arrangements thus are essential in designing, implementing, and maintaining the right incentives. There nevertheless are requirements for documentation to prevent abuses and to provide information on exports. For example, with a free trade regime for export activities and a protected regime for domestic production, exporters could increase their earnings by selling final products or intermediate goods on the domestic market—rather than use those intermediate inputs for export production. To prevent this, the purchases of intermediate inputs are strictly tied to the amount needed to produce the export. And with access to bank loans automatic for export activity, exporters might try to use the funds so acquired for production on the domestic market. So, again, the issuance of loans is strictly tied to the working capital needed to produce the export. The commercial banks and the Bank of Korea administer the export loans, except those handled by the Export-Import Bank for deferred payment by foreign buyers.[2]

To receive short-term loans for the working capital needed for export production, or to have tariff-free access to imported inputs, export producers need three main things: documentation of actual or expected export orders, an input-coefficient certificate, and documentation of the completed exports. Export letters of credit (or other export contracts) that exporters receive from foreign buyers have been used to document actual direct export orders. To document actual orders for indirect exports—that is, intermediate inputs supplied to another Korean firm for its export production or finished goods supplied by one Korean firm to another Korean firm, which exports them—the Koreans have used the domestic letter of credit (domestic L/C). To document expected orders, the Koreans have used records of a firm's past direct and indirect exports.

Unique to Korea, the domestic L/C is the best example of innovation by the Korean export administration. The instrument was introduced in 1965 and has since been crucial in providing automatic short-term export loans for working capital—and unrestricted access to intermediate inputs—for Korean manufacturers that export indirectly through other Korean firms. With a domestic L/C, which is issued by an exporter's bank on the basis of a direct export order, the indirect exporter can qualify for the same incentives as the direct exporter. So can the suppliers of the indirect exporter—and the suppliers of those suppliers—for the part of their production that ultimately will be exported. The domestic L/C thus breaks the usual barriers that limit the provision of export incentives to final exporters. It opens the basic export incentives to all producers. This broadening of the free trade regime has been important in drawing smaller firms into export production in Korea and inducing them to produce goods of international standard.[3]

Direct and indirect exporters also need an input-coefficient certificate and documentation of the completed exports. An input coefficient indicates how much of an input is needed per unit of output and determines the volume of intermediate inputs that can be imported without restriction. The input-coefficient administration—embracing banks, provincial governments, and the Office of Industrial Promotion in the Ministry of Commerce and Industry—publishes a list of these coefficients for most export commodities. The list is long: in 1979, for example, there were input coefficients for roughly 6,000 export commodities and 17,000 import items. The input-coefficient administration also issues the certificates.

Since 1975 the tariff exemptions have been administered under a drawback system: exporters pay tariffs and indirect taxes when importing their intermediate inputs; they receive rebates after documenting the completion of the export. Exemptions previously were granted at the time of the import of intermediate inputs on the basis of actual or expected export orders.

Additional Incentives

The basic incentives in Korea have been the tariff-free access to imported inputs and the access to bank loans for working capital. These automatic incentives, together with the exchange rate, are the foundation of the Korean system of export promotion. There nevertheless have been additional incentives used to reduce the bias against exporting. Most of these incentives are no longer used. They include income tax reductions; the rationing of medium-term and long-term loans for investment; wastage allowances, which were selectively used to spur certain exports by increasing the input coefficients allowable for imported inputs for those exports, thereby giving producers duty-free imports that could be used for production for the domestic market; import-export links, which permitted the import of prohibited or restricted items (mainly luxury goods that could be sold for a high profit) in exchange for exporting specified goods having low profit margins; reduced rates for electricity and rail transport; and tariff exemptions on imports of capital goods.[4] Only a few of these incentives are still in force: most notable among them are tax incentives for overseas marketing, the postshipment export loans by the Korea Export-Import Bank, and a system of export credit insurance and guarantees. There are, in addition, the provision of basic infrastructure to smooth the flow of export goods and the creation of free trade zones and industrial parks. Finally, the Korean Traders Association and the Korea Trade Promotion Corporation promote Korean exports throughout the world on behalf of Korean firms.

The rationing of longer term domestic and foreign loans was, until the early 1980s, one of the most important instruments of government control over private firms. It was effective for three reasons. First, the government controlled the domestic banks to the extent that it was a major shareholder and had the power to appoint managers (the ownership of commercial banks has recently been transferred to the private sector). Second, the government controlled the inflow of foreign capital, which has accounted for a high percentage of the corporate borrowing in Korea. Third, the government, through the Bank of Korea and the Ministry of Finance, has controlled interest rates in the formal banking sector (there has been an active curb market outside that sector). Taking advantage of these loans, Korean firms have been able to expand rapidly. Some firms, such as those in the tire industry, would not have gotten off to such an early and successful start without long-term investment capital at preferential rates. And with very high debt-equity ratios, most firms, particularly the biggest ones, have relied for their continuing success on an open tap for the flow of bank loans for investment capital.[5]

The rationing of longer term bank loans has thus given the government considerable leverage over firms. The government has used this leverage selectively as a carrot to draw firms down new paths of exporting and to export more than they might otherwise have. Credit rationing, then, has been effective in adding to the government's ability to induce firms, particularly large firms, to carry out its policies, especially those for export promotion. If the banks had been privately controlled—say, by large corporations, as in Japan—the country probably would not have achieved as effectively the government's objectives for the growth of exports and the economy.

The automatic access to working capital for export production is one major contribution of Korea's financial system to the country's success in exporting. But in view of the rapid growth of efficient export industries, the rationing of investment capital is another, perhaps equally important, contribution.[6] This is not to say that such rationing was always efficient. Mistakes were made along the way, particularly in the later 1970s, when there was overinvestment in heavy import-substitution industries. But these recent developments should not overshadow the contributions of the Korean financial system to export promotion in the 1960s and 1970s.[7]

What was the quantitative effect of these basic and additional incentives? A look at the real effective exchange rate for exports shows, despite annual fluctuations, that it was fairly stable between the mid-1960s and the mid-1970s.[8] The rate for imports, though lower than that for exports before the mid-1960s, rose to that for exports and ran parallel with it for much of the period. The system of export incentives thus had two important effects. It reassured exporters of the permanence of government policies designed to remove the disincentives to exporting. And it kept the profitability of production for the export market on par with that for the domestic market. The system thus contributed to the export drive by removing the bias against export production and giving exporters just the incentives they needed to be on an equal footing with producers from other countries.

Key Institutional Mechanisms

All very rational and, as it happens, all very efficient. The question naturally arises, Would Korea's incentives have been right and the administrative arrangements for those incentives efficient without some special institutional mechanisms to provide the information for determining and adjusting them? Probably not. At the very least, Korea would have had to find some other institutional mechanisms that would achieve the same end. Two institutional mechanisms have been selected for analysis here: the system of setting export targets and the practice of holding monthly national trade promotion meetings. These two institutions have been important parts of the institutional framework that have helped translate political resolve into bureaucratic resolve. They have also provided information needed for bureaucratic action.

To understand the operation of these mechanisms, it is necessary to have some idea of the synergistic partnership between government and business in Korea. For Korea's incentive system to have been so effective has taken the commitment of the country's political leadership to economic growth. It also has taken an efficient bureaucracy. In Korea, that commitment has been so strong that it did more than foster the efficiency of the bureaucracy. The commitment unified all economic agents in Korea in a common undertaking—the drive to develop through trade—and in the process forged a partnership of firms, banks, bureaus, universities, and provincial governments. Led by the president, and supported by the top economic ministers and the heads of the biggest firms, much of the country was wrapped in the fervor and enthusiasm surrounding the drive to develop through trade. And that partnership goes far beyond the one between government and business, for it also embraces political parties, research and educational institutions, indeed the entire institutional framework in Korea.

There naturally have been many institutional mechanisms to support the inner workings of this partnership. But without two special mechanisms—the system of export targets and the practice of holding monthly trade promotion meetings—or something in their place, it is unlikely that the entire system of export promotion would have been so effective, that the various incentives would have worked as well as they did, and ultimately that Korea's export performance would have been what it has been. In short, the targets and monthly meetings have, in conjunction with the rest of the institutional framework, unified the entire array of export incentives and have been a catalyst for the workings of the synergistic partnership between government and business.

The export targets basically are projections by firms. In aggregate, they show the government what to expect and what the requirements will be for finance, infrastructure, and other activities in support of the export drive. But the targets also serve as incentives to firms because they sometimes are used as an informal basis for providing such incentives as longer term loans. It therefore is in the interest of firms to set and to achieve high targets. The targets in Korea thus differ from those in centrally planned economies, where it often behooves enterprises to have low targets and to surpass them.

The monthly meetings basically are reviews of progress toward the export targets. But chaired by the president and attended by economic ministers and leading businessmen, the monthly meetings regularly bring the country's political leadership face to face with representatives of the main economic agents in the country. And by focusing on progress toward targets, the monthly meetings bring out problems and instill in top bureaucrats the desire to have all proceed well in their domains. And by airing problems, in a forum where efficiency is the watchword, the monthly meetings foster attempts at immediate solutions. The targets and monthly meetings thus do more than make known how firms are doing. They also make known how government agencies are doing.

The monthly meetings have also been the principal formal forum for the negotiation of mixes and levels of conventional incentives. More important, and invisible to the macroeconomist, those monthly meetings have been the principal forum for the negotiation of administrative arrangements for those incentives. Representatives of export associations or heads of the big firms, when asked at one of the monthly meetings about problems in dealing with the incentives bureaucracy, would invariably push for a reduction in the restrictions and other barriers that keep some incentives out of the reach of some firms. And invariably there would be pressure put on the banks and government agencies to simplify requirements for paperwork. And just as invariably there would be resistance from an agency that is as concerned about preventing abuses as it is about extending the benefits associated with the incentives.

The system of export targets and the practice of holding monthly trade promotion meetings have also, in concert with the political leadership's commitment to exporting, enabled the use of unconventional export incentives on top of the conventional incentives already described. Some of these have operated through formal channels. Public exhortations by the president about the importance of exporting and public awards by the president and other notables at the monthly meetings are examples of the unconventional incentives that have imbued the export drive with a powerful team spirit and simultaneously unleashed the natural competitive spirit of the heads of firms. Exporters are assigned to many categories of export performance, and because of the public attention to the category a firm is in, most exporters strive to be in the highest. Added to this are awards of the national medal of honor and other presidential citations to the most successful of the big exporters. And dangling as carrots for other exporters is an array of awards for having broken new ground in exporting. Such incentives would have little effect in many parts of the world, but in Korea they are taken very seriously—not only because of the recognition associated with them, but because of the economic rewards that may follow.

Other carrots and sticks have operated informally, such as the president's telephone calls to the heads of the larger firms. The story of Hyundai's reluctant entry into shipbuilding after first having balked is the best known: the company turned out two world-class tankers thirty months after breaking ground for their presidentially inspired shipyard in 1973 (Jones and Sakong 1980, pp. 119–20). But there have also been numerous similar instances, each of them carrying implications, if not assurances, of government support. These presidential sticks, combined with prospective carrots, have affected the activities of the largest firms.

Another set of unconventional incentives, also operated informally, is that of encouraging firms to export in the early stages of production of goods for sale on the domestic market. Using this very selectively, the Korean government was able to spur some of the big firms to start up more new lines of export production than would otherwise have been possible.[9] And by so doing, the government was able to avoid the inefficiency that so often permanently plagues infant industries. But to manage the informal system of encouraging exports in the early stages of production, the government needed some institutional mechanisms to link export sales to domestic production. The system of export targets and monthly meetings provided this link.

In understanding Korea's success in exporting, it thus is necessary to look beyond the obvious:

- It is necessary to look beyond the automatic export incentives to the administrative arrangements for those incentives.
- It is necessary to look beyond the usual bureaucratic mechanisms to the special mechanisms contributing to the synergistic partnership of business and government, such mechanisms as the system of setting export targets and the practice of holding monthly trade promotion meetings.
- It is necessary to look beyond conventional incentives to such unconventional incentives as presenting presidential citations and encouraging exports at an early stage of production.
- It is necessary to look beyond formal channels of granting incentives to informal channels not codified in rules and regulations.

It also is necessary to look beyond the products and production methods chosen by firms to the ways they acquire and master technology and market their products overseas.

Notes to Chapter 2

1. For theoretical justification of infant industry protection, see McKinnon (1971, 1979); for empirical justification, Westphal (1981, 1982b) and Shinohara (1982). For the

infeasibility of floating exchange rates for most developing countries, see Lewis (1977) and McKinnon (1981).

2. See Rhee (1984) for details of the administrative and banking procedures for receiving export loans and for importing intermediate inputs to be used in export production.

3. For example, a survey of firms in 1979 showed that roughly 40 percent of Korea's direct and indirect exports were by small and medium-size firms. The domestic L/C system has thus helped in the development of small indirect exporters through efficient backward linkages from direct exporters. See Rhee (1984).

4. For details on the various incentives used in Korea, see Westphal and Kim (1977) and Suh (1981).

5. In Japan, too, firms have traditionally financed their operations primarily through bank loans, not through stock and bond markets, as firms in the other developed countries have done (Bronte 1982; Shinohara 1982).

6. For further discussion of the positive side of Korea's credit rationing system, see Mason and others (1980, p. 340) and Jones and Sakong (1980, pp. 101–10).

7. See Cole and Park (1983) for a similar view.

8. In 1965 prices that rate was 286.1 won per dollar in 1964 and 285.1 per dollar in 1974. See Westphal and Kim (1977, pp. 1–13 to 1–18). The real effective exchange rate for exports adjusts the official rate to take into account tax and other incentives and the difference between domestic inflation and world inflation.

9. See Westphal and Kim (1977), p. 3–55.

3

Key Institutions

MAINTAINING THE BASIC AUTOMATIC INCENTIVES for export promotion is not
an easy task, as chapter 2 makes clear. The administrative arrangements essential for guaranteeing exporters access to those incentives
have to be adjusted in response to continuing evaluations of effectiveness of the incentive system. The information needed for these
adjustments must be sought and sifted. In Korea some of the most
important information needed for such adjustments comes from the
process of setting export targets and holding monthly national trade
promotion meetings. True, many other institutional mechanisms
have been processing economic information in Korea. We focus on
these two institutions because they are particularly suited to exporting, to the Korean temperament, and to the Korean situation. They
also do more than process information.

In this chapter we examine the responses of firms to questions
about the export targets and monthly trade promotion meetings. The
purpose is to put some flesh on hitherto bare bones in the literature
about the importance and nature of such institutions. We also spell
out some of the contributions of these institutions to the export drive
through their effect on the efficiency of processing information and
administering incentives.[1]

Export Targets

The government initiated the system of setting export targets in the
early 1960s, an idea they probably picked up from the Japanese (Johnson 1982, pp. 229–30). At first, the government issued export targets
to firms. The heads of firms, with the memory still fresh of their being
jailed by the new regime for the illicit accumulation of wealth, were
inclined to comply. But even then the communication went both

ways: the heads of some of the larger firms were asked on their release to submit recommendations about what they needed to help them export (Jones and Sakong 1980). That started the dialogue between government and firms about exporting and about the incentives needed to support production for export.

Although allocated in the early 1960s by the government from the top down, targets have mainly been set by the exporting firms with the cooperation and approval of export associations and the government. As firms grew, and as the government began to rely increasingly on firms for information needed in planning, the government began more and more to coordinate targets while firms initiated them. Only firms had the detailed information about international markets and their change. But government ministries, the government's representatives overseas (especially embassies), each industry's export association, and the broader trade organization all have had an important hand in the system.

The annual targets are set for firms, commodities, industries, and overseas markets. The targets are broken down by quarter and by month, and firm-level targets cover indirect exports (under the domestic letters of credit described in chapter 2) as well as direct exports. In 1962 the national target was $61.9 million, and exports were $5 million short of that. In 1976, the year of our survey, the export target was $6.5 billion—a hundred times the first target—and that was surpassed by $1.2 billion. In 1978 the national target was up to $12.5 billion; in 1981, to $21.5 billion (see figure 3–1).

The head of the export promotion office in the Ministry of Commerce and Industry has at his side a computer printout of progress against targets by industry and by firm. The data is for the preceding day, which is all the more remarkable when it is considered that most developing countries do not have aggregate information on exports for many months. That printout is also broken down by geographic region. If sales in a region are not up to target, the Korean ambassadors there are recalled to find out what the problems are and what can be done to spur Korean sales. And in the foyer of the head office of the Korean Trader's Association is a big board tracking the progress of each industry toward its target. The export associations of each industry, the nodes for all information flows on exports, have their own boards tracking progress. So do firms on the shop floors, where workers—dressed in uniforms that give all of industry a paramilitary air—keep track of their firm's progress toward targets and of that by competitors down the street.

Figure 3-1.   *Annual Export Targets and Annual Export Performance*

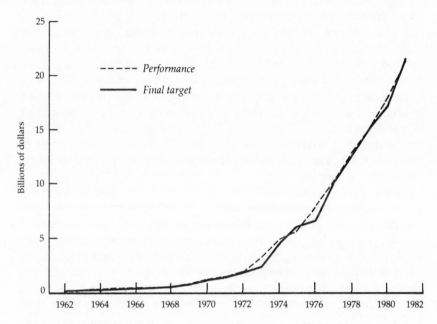

Source: Appendix table B-5.

Setting targets

Once a year the export manager of a large firm, or the head of a smaller firm, works with his staff to determine what the value of their exports will be for the coming year. Most of the firms surveyed, five in six, indicated that their annual export target was their own estimate, which sometimes was adjusted by the government (see A-3 in appendix A). As a basis for that estimate, the firms used one or a combination of three methods: extrapolating their past export growth; considering their capacity, with allowances for the growth of domestic demand; estimating the growth of demand for each of their important export products (A-5). For one firm in six the targets were either a share of an industrywide target agreed on by the firm's export association and the government or a target assigned by the government on the basis of past performance (A-3).

The way firms establish targets differs from one industry to the next (A-6). Some firms, such as many of those in the nylon industry and the worsted wool industry, simply submit their targets to their industry's export association, which assembles the targets and passes them on to the Ministry of Commerce and Industry. Firms in some other industries discuss targets with the other ministries they must deal with—such as Construction or Agriculture and Forestry. Still others have targets set for them by the Ministry of Commerce and Industry—on the basis, say, of past performance and growth rates or of quantitative restrictions importing countries have put on Korean products. The pattern—if there is one—seems to be this: Mature firms in mature industries set their own targets or work out the targets with their industry's export associations and with the ministries. Firms in newer industries or in industries affected by import quotas have their targets set for them.

In all but a few firms the top executives spent fewer than ten man-days on work associated with the targets (A–7). Administrative personnel spent fewer than ten man-days in half the firms, more than ten in the other half (and more than fifty in an eighth). Firms were split on whether the time and effort preparing and discussing targets were moderate or considerable, except for the tenth that found them negligible. For large firms the forecasting is part of normal planning and administration and probably is seen as requiring moderate time and effort. For smaller firms, with scarce managerial resources, the time and effort are seen as being more considerable.

Do firms try to set their targets low, given the difficulty and uncertainty in exporting? Or high, given the expectation of benefits associated with good export performance? We have no evidence on this, but the following speculations seem reasonable. Militating against a firm's deliberately setting low targets is the team mentality and competitive temperament of Koreans. So, setting a low target, or not reaching a target, would in many senses be letting down the team, whichever team it might be: the people in the firm as a team, the firms in the industry as a team, the industries in the country as a team. Even if a firm were not overly competitive, it would strive to reach or at least come close to its target. There would be little pressure on such an uncompetitive firm to perform well if all other firms in the industry are performing poorly, but that pressure rises considerably if other firms in the industry are reaching and exceeding their targets (as almost always happened).

The competition in an industry for sales must carry over to the competition in an industry for targets—they are synonymous, one for the present, one the future. A firm may even want to be number one—because of what that means for prestige and for special consideration in future dealings with the government. So the tendency is for some firms to come up with a target somewhat larger than they might set alone. Other firms might be content to let others in the industry come up with big targets for the (often less profitable) export market. But they would then miss out on some of the benefits that might be expected to go along with exporting.

The way targets are set makes it hard for firms to set them either too high or too low. First, the export associations would bounce a proposed target back to the firm if it is out of line with past production or the targets of other firms. Second, the Ministry of Commerce and Industry bounces a firm's (or industry's) proposed target back if it is out of line with past production, with other industries, or with the government's priorities for resource allocation. Moreover, the ministers will not accept exceedingly high targets for fear of being sacked or called on the carpet if the targets are not met. Nor will the ministers accept unambitious targets, because that could get them sacked just as easily. Such feelings run through the bureaucracy.

Revising targets

The export targets are revised to take into account circumstances not foreseen or performance better than envisioned. Almost a third of the firms had a target revised during 1973–75 (A–2). Firms most frequently mentioned the world recession—and its concomitants: higher energy prices, slackened orders, and stagnant markets—as the reason for having a target revised downward in 1973–76. The firms also mentioned production shortfalls, delays in plant expansion, and excessive original targets. For upward revisions of targets, firms mentioned the recovery from recession most frequently; they also mentioned expansions of operations, improvements in the ability to export, and unexpected increases in orders for their products. The revisions explain why the average differences between average targets and average performance in 1973–75 were small (A–1).

That the government and the firms take the export targets seriously is evident in the congruence of performance with those targets, especially the revised targets (see figure 3–2). If the object of the targets had been sheer propaganda, the government and firms would have looked better by stacking performance against the initial targets, which almost always were exceeded. If the object had been sheer information, the government could have gathered it simply by following reports of past and expected performance. But because of the frequent updating of targets during the year, the main objects clearly

Figure 3–2.   *Export Performance in Relation to Final Export Targets*

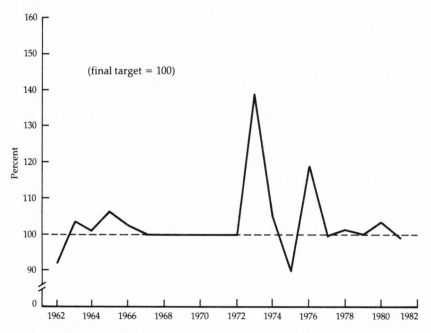

Source: Appendix table B–5.

have been to keep the targets realistic (so that they would continue to be taken seriously), to spur as much as possible the national effort to export, and to obtain not merely information but the best information possible. The targets thus are tough enough to stimulate competition between firms, but they also are flexible enough to be revised when circumstances beyond the control of the firm or country change.

Reaching targets

For half the firms in the survey, reaching targets called for a special effort but no big changes in plans, such as unplanned capacity expansions (A–4). A third said targets could easily be achieved or surpassed in 1975, which was not a boom year for Korean exports. The rest said that they had to embark on a big expansion, on a reorganization, or on both—in addition to changes planned. And a few firms (ten in 1975 and one in 1976) complained that the targets were unreasonable and beyond their abilities.

1975 and one in 1976) complained that the targets were unreasonable and beyond their abilities.

Three firms in five said that they had failed to meet at least one of their targets during 1973–75 (see A–14). Such failures are not evident in figure 3–2, which gives only the average performance of all firms. The reasons mentioned most frequently for not meeting targets had their origin outside Korea: the oil shock, the world recession, the competition from other countries, the changes in fashion in principal markets, the quantitative restrictions other countries imposed on Korea's exports, the increases in the cost of raw materials in the face of flagging demand (A–14). Also frequently mentioned was that the original targets were too high, generally because the firm's share of quotas was too limiting or because production capacity either was insufficient or inefficient (say, if a big expansion were under way). Other reasons include shortages of raw materials (for a plywood company), a poor catch (for fishing companies), shortages in supply due to a rise in domestic sales, delays in the development of new products, and the upward revision of an original target that had already been (or would be) passed.

Firms responded variously to the question, Why is reaching export targets important? Mentioned most often were the recognition accorded them by government ministries and the pride from doing well in comparison with their competitors (A–8). Some big firms may have gone overboard in meeting or exceeding targets because of the desire to be the number one company in an industry. It seems, too, that some big firms would suffer short-term losses in the expectation of long-term advantages, such as preferential treatment in the rationing of loans for capacity expansion and in the bureaucratic support needed for the firm's day-to-day operations. Some companies, just to be number one in their industry, would buy up the orders and sales of smaller companies at a premium or in exchange with promises of technical advice and other favors.

Effect of targets

The targets, because of the way they are set and revised, have the appearance of mere projections. Not so, for although they are projections in the strict sense, they generally are ambitious projections, higher than what a firm would otherwise project in the absence of expectations for formal and informal incentives and the competition and extraordinary effort stirred up among firms. As such, the targets are true targets, not merely projections. That this is so is evidenced in what firms said about the effect of targets on their production. Half the firms said the targets increased their production more rapidly than was planned in 1974 and 1975; three-fifths of the firms in 1976 (A–10). Only a twentieth of them said that targets made no difference to their production in 1974, but a quarter said the targets made no difference in 1975, not an unusually good year for Korean exports. For production in 1976 the proportion of firms that said the targets made no difference was back down to a seventh, and that was for performance during only the first half of the year, when targets have their weakest bite. About a quarter of the firms responded that production for the domestic market had to be forestalled or forgone to meet targets for the export market in each of those three years. Also mentioned as effects of target-setting were reductions in profitability—because of price cutting, unprofitable exports, and increased unit costs.

In assessing the advantages of good export performance, the firms identified continuing government support of their export activity as most important (A–11). That support subsumes all automatic incentives and all discretionary incentives and penalties. The response indicates the importance of the export target-setting in the bargaining between the government and the export firms and their associations.[2] That support also relates to a firm's dealings with government agencies. Two firms in five said that good export performance facilitated those dealings (A–12). For example, permission to work with foreign firms, to import technology, to bring in foreign consultants, to send employees overseas for training—permission to do these things and many others must come from the appropriate ministry. Firms with good export records get their approvals faster—as part of the national policy of helping first and most the firms that are doing well, and the firms that are doing well are generally the successful exporters. Three firms in five said that the rigor with which government audited their tax returns depended on their export performance (A–12).

The firms also attached considerable importance to the advantages of good export performance for getting the government's support of capacity expansion. The government, through its control of the banking system and of inflows of foreign financial resources, controls the allocation of long-term loans. Its practice is to make sure that successful firms are the first to get what they needed—with success frequently measured by exports. Firms that do not meet their targets are farther down the queue, and they know it.

Monthly National Trade Promotion Meetings

Setting and revising targets is one thing. Monitoring progress toward them is another. At the very least, the government has had to know how firms were doing in relation to expectation and in relation to other firms. But to promote exports effectively, it had to know—if firms were doing poorly—what they were doing wrong and what could be done to help them out. It had to know—if conditions changed—what those changes meant for the activities of firms and for the incentives and other support it proffered them. Similarly, firms had to know the government's plans for the economy, for different sectors, and for changes in policy. Gathering and disseminating such information naturally was part of the daily routine of the economic ministries, given the commitment to exporting. Needed, however, was a regular forum for such exchanges of information beyond the usual exchanges between ministries.

The first National Export Promotion Meeting, later to be called the National Trade Promotion Meeting, was held in 1965. The monthly meetings have since provided a forum for exchanges of information between firms and the many agencies of government involved in the export drive. About that same time, President Park Chung Hee became much more adamant about the importance of exporting to the survival of the nation, and the monthly meetings provided one context for his exhortations. The monthly meetings quickly became the focal point of the Korean export drive.

Participants and agendas

Chaired by the president, the monthly trade promotion meetings are select gatherings of the ministers and top bureaucrats responsible for trade and the economy; the chief executives of export associations, research organizations, and educational institutions; and the heads of a few firms, mainly the general trading companies and other large firms (see figure 3-3). The prominence of those attending shows that the monthly meetings are far more than perfunctory meetings to improve coordination between the private and public sectors. Of the firms in the sample, which were much larger than average Korean firms, about half said that they had attended at least one meeting during 1974-76, about a third that they had attended more than five meetings a year (A-16). The pattern for two-thirds of the firms was to be regularly represented by their export association. Most of them

Figure 3–3. *Attendants at the Monthly Trade Promotion Meeting in June 1976*

The president
Eleven economic and political staff of the president
Eighteen cabinet ministers
Three ambassadors
(to Kuwait, Saudi Arabia, and United Arab Emirates)
Eighteen assistant ministers of key economic ministries
Thirty-eight bureau chiefs and other staff of economic ministries
Ten representatives of local governments
Four representatives of the national assembly
Two representatives of the ruling party
Eight representatives of commercial and government banks
Five representatives of government and private research institutes
Four representatives of universities
Thirty-nine representatives of industry, trade, and export associations
Eleven representatives of firms

took part in discussions about the agenda of the monthly meeting at their export association before and after the meeting: before, to send up their progress and requirements; after, to find out about the response of government and the policy signals it was sending (A–17). Export associations also send out regular circulars to keep their members apprised of the goings on at the monthly meetings (A–18).

The moderator of the typical monthly meeting is a minister, usually of Finance, of Foreign Affairs, or of Commerce and Industry. The first item on the agenda is a briefing by the moderator on progress toward targets and on problems encountered (see figure 3–4). Then the president comments, perhaps designating some ministry to look into something, perhaps resolving the matter by executive fiat on the spot. For example, at one meeting the export association for the construction industry submitted a list of problems. One of these was that firms in the industry did not get the same income tax rebate that other exporters did. The president decided on the spot to give it to them.

Such treatment of problems, at the highest level, has created an environment geared to rapid solutions. It also keeps bureaucrats on their toes, for they have to be ready with answers to the president's questions. That can wreak havoc in the routine work of a bureaucracy, but it certainly gives bureaucrats signals, resounding once a month, that exporting is what is important. That has made bureaucratic action more important in Korea than bureaucratic rules and rigidities.

Also on the agenda of each meeting are subjects of special interest. For example, at one meeting in 1976 there was an analysis of the effects in the short and long terms of developments in the trade relations between Japan and China and a presentation of the government's strategy for competing with Chinese exports. The more usual focus, however, is on the progress and problems of one industry.

After the briefing and discussion of one special issue, there usually is a ceremony to present citations and medals. After that ceremony, there may be a small trade show, with all in attendance going through an exhibit of, say, the new products of the mechanical engineering industry. Or there may be a visit to a new factory. Then the president hosts a lunch for his ministers and the heads of the biggest firms.

Export Day

When Korea's exports passed $100 million on 30 November 1964, the milestone was marked by declaring Export Day, which has been celebrated every year since. The focus of the celebration is the award of prizes at a large public gathering, prizes that the heads of firms take seriously (A–13). There are president's prizes for being the number one exporter in an industry, for export merit as a small or medium-size firm, for exceeding a target by more than 50 percent. There are prime minister's prizes for inventions, for excellence in design, for having a high reputation in exhibitions overseas, or for developing an export product of high quality. And there are prizes for reaching a certain level of exports. There are, in addition, industry medals and prizes awarded by various ministries.

The award of these prizes is akin to the pinning of medals on officers—with salutes, solemnity, and sharp strides. The heads of firms typically display the awards in their offices—along with a picture of the president and calligraphy inscribed to the head of the firm and carrying messages on the importance of exporting. Here, for example, are the awards that Daewoo received between 1968 and the time of the survey in 1976: the president's prize in November 1968, the iron tower in 1970, the bronze tower in 1971, the golden tower in 1974, the president's prize again in 1973, the $100 million export tower in 1974, and the president's banner for special export merit in 1975 (A–13).

On Export Day in 1981, more than 600 prizes were awarded in celebrating Korea's having passed the $20 billion mark in exporting.

Figure 3–4. *Agendas for the Monthly Trade Promotion Meetings, 1974*

Month	Agenda
January	• Export targets for 1974 • Detailed implementation program for export promotion policies • Analysis of inefficiency in the export incentive administration
February	• Analysis of export performance through January • Report on major administrative matters related to export promotion • Status of the import-export administration of local governments and its improvement
March	• Analysis of export performance through February • Results of the meeting with the New Zealand commerce minister and of the special raw materials mission to New Zealand • Policies for construction exports • Reforms of import financing and raw materials administration • Public campaign for export promotion
April	• Analysis of export performance through March • Report on major administrative matters related to export promotion • Letter-of-credit arrivals and causes for bad export records for certain commodities • Results of the annual conference of Korean ambassadors and chiefs of overseas missions in Asia • International picture of import restrictions for textile products
May	• Analysis of export performance through April • Report on major administrative matters related to export promotion

Month	Agenda
May	• Export performance of joint-venture companies • Status of the foreign trade of mainland China
June	• Analysis of export performance through May • Status and projections of Korea's exports to Japan • Measures to promote exports of silk products • Status of tie exports
August	• Analysis of export performance through July • Report on China's exhibition in Osaka • Status of the Pohang steel mill
September	• Analysis of export performance through August • Reform of system of quality inspection for exports • Measures to promote selected major export commodities • Policies to accelerate exports
October	• Analysis of export performance through September • Status of U.S. textile import restrictions against Korea • Status of shipping costs and measures to reduce them • Status of Saemaul Movement factories
November	• Analysis of export performance and letter-of-credit arrival through October • Report on Korea's overseas exhibitions of export commodities • Analysis of effect of exporting on economic linkages to other domestic industries • Report on the awards at the 11th Export Day
December	• Analysis of export performance in 1974 • Export targets for 1975 • Comprehensive export promotion policies for 1975

Note: There was no meeting in July.
Source: Korea (1974).

These included three $1.5 billion towers, two $500 million towers, sixteen $100 million towers, thirteen $50 million towers, fifty-four $10 million towers, three gold medals, three silver medals, three bronze medals, six iron medals, twenty-three tin medals, eighty other industrial medals, 122 presidential citations, 120 prime minister's citations, and 204 citations from the Ministry of Commerce and Industry.

Effect of monthly meetings

The importance of the monthly trade promotion meetings and the attention assigned to them have been commensurate with the size of exports and industry. The process of setting and revising targets and monitoring progress toward them kept getting stronger because of the importance of exports to the economy and to the nation. By the mid-1970s the monthly meetings were one of the most publicized events in Korea: ministries were constantly preparing for them; the press frequently reporting on them.

What was the effect of the meetings? More than three-fifths of the firms considered the meetings to have significantly affected their export performance during 1974–76 (A–21). The meetings would have done this in two ways: through the exhortations to meet and exceed targets; through the accommodations by government to help firms in their efforts to export. For the firms that said the meetings affected their export performance, considerable weight was given to the importance of the meetings in resolving difficulties or delays in the firms' dealings with government ministries and to decisions of principle that affected exporting. Also important were identifying important issues and problems and getting information in preparing for meetings or in attending them. The meetings thus contributed much to the flexibility of Korea's policies for export promotion, and to their rapid adjustment. Just as firms have been the agents of government's larger objectives, so the bureaus are the agents, within limits, of helping the firms achieve targets.

How strong was the pressure the monthly meetings put on firms to have a good export performance? Attention devoted to the meetings in the media each month, and the big splash on Export Day, made certain that meetings were in the minds of chief executives and export managers whether they attended or not. More than a third of the firms said the pressure was considerable; about a half, moderate or slight; the rest, little or none (A–19). The pressure was of two kinds: one, the pressure that the meetings put on firms directly—to meet targets; two, the pressure that the firms put on themselves—to do better than or as well as their principal competitors. That two-thirds of the firms did not find the pressure of the meetings considerable may show that the greater function of the meetings had been informational—and that much of the pressure to have good export performance came not from the meetings, but from the export associations and from the firms themselves.

Part of what makes the targets effective, in addition to their simply being set, is the monthly reminder of how firms and industries are progressing toward them. And part of what makes the monthly meetings effective, in addition to their ritualized regularity, is that there is something tangible and current to discuss—the progress toward targets and the impediments to that progress. The information uncovered by the meetings prompts changes not only in targets but in the policies and administrative arrangements for export incentives. What really makes the monthly meetings effective, of course, is that they have a track record of serving the primary interests of the government (export-led economic growth) and the firms (profit).

Contributions to the Export Drive

The export targets and monthly meetings provide some of the most important information needed to administer the Korean export drive. Perhaps most important is the up-to-date information on export performance by firm, product, and market and on reasons for discrepancy between targets and performance. The government also gets much solid information about what is going on in the world. (The firms, meanwhile, get much solid information about the priorities and undertakings by government.) But the government has not only acquired this information. It has acted wisely on the information. The ministries, in concert with the firms, have sought first to identify problems and opportunities and to determine appropriate actions. These actions have been characterized by:

- Pragmatism. The government has been willing to try any methods that might achieve the desired ends.
- Speed. The government has preferred the immediate implementation of policies that might work to the delayed implementation of policies that would definitely work only after much protracted study.
- Flexibility. The government has been willing to modify its policies and programs and to retreat from mistakes—something essential when new policies are speedily implemented.

These characteristics of bureaucratic decision-making have enabled the government to use the information flowing from the export targets and monthly meetings to adjust policy with great decisiveness and refinement. The characteristics were fostered by the political leadership's single-minded commitment to exporting as the engine of economic growth. They were also fostered by the capabilities of the bureaucracy and the close relations between firms and government. They were fostered, too, by the team mentality and corresponding competitiveness of the Korean export drive: all ministries and firms have been part of the team, and if one member wandered astray, others would reign the wanderer back in.

As Jones and Sakong have noted: "The Korean policy-making style is not so much a deliberate one of careful planning and debate, but more one of diving in, getting started, observing results, adjusting policy, and repeating the process until the appropriate mix is found" (1980, p.293). For example, when balance-of-payments problems worsened in 1975, the government hastily proposed replacing the system of prior tariff exemptions for export producers by a system of having firms pay duties on their intermediate inputs and then draw them back after completing the export. That threatened to increase the antiexport bias, and when firms and export associations expressed concern about the effect the new system would have on their exports, the government introduced corrective measures that would reduce the antiexport bias.[3] This willingness to implement new policies without careful, deliberate planning was generally a virtue for export policy-making—primarily because the test of those policies was success on the international marketplace. Firms thus saw the flexibility and frequent adjustments in the incentive system not as characteristics that would create uncertainty about the automaticity and stability of that system. They saw them as part of the government's long-term commitment to keep exports profitable—a commitment made possible by the continuity of government. Without such a commitment, without such continuity, firms would have faced much more uncertainty in their export production, and exports would have suffered as a result. We will discuss in chapter 6 the problems of heavy industry planning during the later 1970s, when policy-makers put the objective of import substitution in heavy industry alongside that of export promotion.

In addition to providing information needed to administer the system of export incentives, the targets and monthly meetings fulfill some other important functions:

- They focus the activities of government agencies on the promotion and administration of exports.
- They focus the activities of firms on exporting and the attention of firms on how well they are doing in relation to other exporters.
- They provide a forum for the government and the firms (or their trade associations) to negotiate the levels of incentives and their administrative arrangements.
- They provide a forum for the government to operate some unconventional incentives through formal channels (awards and citations) and the information needed to operate other unconventional incentives through informal channels.
- Thus they help to unify the whole system of export incentives and the entire exporting effort.
- They also provide grist for the government's public campaign about the role of exporting in the future of the nation.

The system of export targets and the practice of holding monthly meetings thus are two important institutions for forging the synergistic partnership of government and business. They consequently have some manipulative aspects: the president manipulates ministries and firms, the ministries manipulate firms, and the firms try to manipulate ministries.

The government has used this manipulative side of the targets and monthly meetings, indeed the entire institutional setup for the export drive, judiciously. The across-the-board exhortations to firms rallied them around the export drive and the country's survival. The selective urging of firms to export in the early stages of production for the domestic market may have led the big firms to occasional mistakes and inefficiencies in the short run, but the overall outcome seems to have been an array of new successful ventures that otherwise would not have been initiated and a higher degree of efficiency stemming from the need to be competitive in international markets. Even the occasional mistakes and inefficiencies could be tolerated because of the bureaucracy's responsiveness to new information and willingness to retreat from policies failing to yield desired results. As long as the manipulative side of the Korean institutional setup was selectively mediated by ministries and directed at exporting, it would generally lead to efficient choices by firms.

Did the target-setting and monthly meetings make a difference in the Korean export drive? It is almost impossible to say no. It can be hypothesized, for example, that without the targets, without the monthly meetings, and without the forums and flows of information—that without these things (or something in their place) export growth and economic growth would both have been slower. What must be made clear, however, is that these two mechanisms cannot simply be tacked onto the institutional arrangements of any country. They have worked in Korea in large part because of the fervor the government has stirred around the export drive and because of the prospects firms have had for profit for taking part in that drive.

Notes to Chapter 3

1. Arrow (1974a) argues that inequality in economic development is associated, among other things, with differences in informational efficiency. Hurwicz (1973) asserts the importance of informational efficiency and incentive compatibility in designing mechanisms for resource allocation. For more on organizations as processors of information, see Arrow (1974b) as well.
2. See Westphal (1978), p. 376.
3. See Rhee (1980).

4

Selectivity in Technology

ACQUIRING THE TECHNOLOGY NEEDED for export production and accumulating the capability to use that technology effectively and adapt it in ways that maintain a firm's international competitiveness call for much more than buying a machine and flipping a switch. The reason is that technology is much more than a machine to be turned on and off. It is a complex array of procedures needed for the design and operation of products, processes, plants, and organizations. Which of these procedures are originated locally—and which purchased from abroad—is in large part determined by the technological capability that has been accumulated by the individual, the firm, and the country. That capability, in turn, comes from more than experience in production. It comes, in addition, from conscious efforts to adapt, assimilate, and create technology.

Such technological efforts often must originate in the strategy of a firm (or country). A firm might decide, in the absence of such a strategy, to have a foreign company come in and build it a turnkey plant at the largest scale possible. Another firm might decide, under such a strategy, to have a foreign company build it a turnkey plant at a much smaller scale—with the provision that its technicians be trained in a way that would equip them to undertake a growing number of tasks in successive expansions of capacity.

In this chapter we analyze the responses of firms to questions about the technology for their most important products. In the first section we describe the selectivity of firms in turning to different sources for their technology. In the second we examine the way firms selectively added to their technological capability. We conclude by speculating about the advantages of the course that Korean firms followed.

Figure 4-1. *Sources of Technology for Korean Firms*

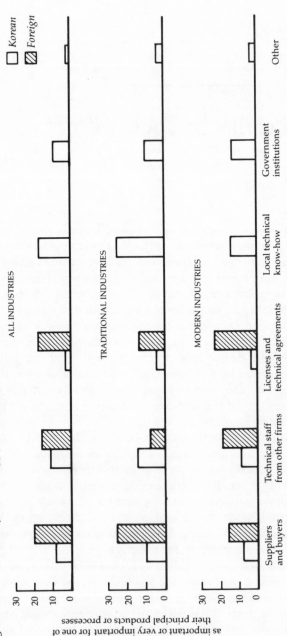

Percentage of firms regarding a source
as important or very important for one of
their principal products or processes

Note: Each firm determined the technology or technologies for which the importance of different sources was indicated; 88 firms responded with respect to 241 technologies. The frequencies are not weighted by the scale or value of the products or processes and thus are not quantitative indicators in these respects. In other words, they show how many firms found a source to be important, not how important firms felt a source to be. We nevertheless believe that the frequencies broadly identify the important sources and ways of acquiring technology. The traditional industries include toys, wigs, shoes, cement, plywood, clothing, textiles, handcrafts, fresh fish, processed food, leather goods, and sporting goods, among others. The modern industries include tableware, electronics, refined sugar, transport equipment, construction services, nonelectrical machinery, basic metal products, and synthetic fibers and resins, among others.

Source: Appendix table A–22.

Sources of Technology

Where did Korea get most of its technology in the first half of the 1970s? The sources that exporting firms identified about half the time as being important for their principal products and processes were Korean (figure 4–1).[1] Much of the technology obtained from Korean sources originally was foreign, but it had been so adapted and assimilated as to be considered Korean. Foreign sources were more important for modern industries than for traditional industries, but not much more.[2] And Korean sources were regarded as important more frequently by traditional firms, but not much more frequently. These results may be attributable to the absence in our sample of technology-intensive modern industries—and they may become increasingly inapplicable as the share of such industries increases in Korean exports.

Of the various categories of sources, buyers of output and suppliers of capital equipment and raw materials were cited as being important most frequently—more than a quarter of the time. Korea's rapidly growing volume of exports and its location on the East Asian circuit help explain why these buyers and suppliers figured so prominently. Suppliers were more important than buyers, but only slightly more; foreign buyers and suppliers were considerably more important than Korean buyers and suppliers. The important thing about foreign buyers, many of which have offices in Seoul, is that they do much more than buy and specify. The same is true, though less so, of foreign suppliers. Foreign buyers and suppliers provide access to information about what product styles are wanted and about how to make products of a desired style. They come in, too, with models and patterns for Korean engineers to follow, and they even go out to the production line to teach workers how to do things.

The second most important source of technology, almost as important as the first, was technical staff with experience in other firms. Such transfers of labor were ranked as an important source slightly less than a quarter of the time. Once again, Korean sources were more important than foreign sources for traditional industries, less important for modern industries.

Licensing and technical agreements were cited as being important about a fifth of the time. Further disaggregation would show licensing, which receives so much attention in discussions of the acquisition of technology by developing countries, to have been considered important in fewer than a tenth of the cases. It was no more important than the information supplied by the two main government institutes, the Korea Institute of Science and Technology and the Korea Science and Technology Information Center.

Local technical know-how was also cited as being important about a fifth of the time. This know-how is not only that traditional to Korea in the sense of being well established; it also covers technology that may have come from foreign sources fairly recently but that firms felt to be well absorbed. Local technical know-how is similar to Atkinson and Stiglitz's localized technology (1969), Katz's "incremental, locally generated technological knowledge" (1978, p. 9), and the idiosyncratic technology discussed in Westphal and others (1984). Technical assistance from Korean buyers and Korean suppliers of capital equipment and raw materials were considered to be an important source about a tenth of the time, as were government-supported research institutes and information services. Licenses from Korean firms and technical assistance from Korean affiliates were not important.

Of the foreign sources, licenses from abroad and technical assistance from foreign affiliates were considered to be important only about a sixth of the time, or less frequently than technical assistance from all other foreign sources. This finding contradicts a hypothesis often put forward (for example, by Brash 1966) but not yet tested: that informal or semiformal transfers associated with direct foreign investment tend to substitute for licensing, so that if direct foreign investment is low, as it is in Korea, licenses will account for a high share of transfers.

Two examples show the kinds of product and process for which foreign and Korean sources have differed in their importance. A big textile company said that traditional Korean know-how and technical assistance of Korean machine suppliers were important as sources for the technology for producing cotton yarn. Compare those sources— for a traditional product made since colonial times—with the ones for acrylic yarn, a newer product: technical staff with experience in foreign factories and technical assistance of foreign machinery suppliers. For the design of ships, a modern product, the following sources were important: technical staff with experience in foreign shipyards, technical assistance from foreign companies, and licensing from foreign firms. But for less complicated tasks of production engineering, all the important sources were Korean: traditional Korean know-how and technical assistance from Korean suppliers, Korean parent companies, and Korean joint-venture partners.

The disaggregation of responses by industry is reported in appendix A (A–22–1 through A–22–4). For most industries in the traditional sector, local technical know-how and technical staff who previously worked for other Korean producers were the most important domestic sources (A–22–2). Of the foreign sources for these industries, licenses were less important than either technical assistance from foreign buyers or that from foreign suppliers of capital equipment and raw materials. Government-supported research institutes and information services were about equal in importance to technical staff who worked in foreign factories. In the resource-based traditional industries, local technical know-how was very important, but they differ on other sources (A–22–3). The fishing industry relied heavily on foreign buyers, the cement industry on foreign suppliers of capital equipment and on technical staff who worked in foreign factories.

For industries in the modern sector, the broad findings were much the same as for those in the traditional sector, with these exceptions (A–22–4):

- The importance of technical staff who had worked in foreign firms was greater.
- The importance of licenses from foreign firms was greater.
- The importance of foreign affiliates was greater—which is attributable to the greater amount of direct foreign investment, principally in electronics.
- The importance of government-supported research institutes and information services was greater, if still moderate—which is attributable to the attention paid to modern industry, to the exclusion of traditional industry.
- The importance of foreign buyers was less (except in tableware).

None of these findings is surprising.

Of the foreign origins of technology, Korean exporters have been relying most heavily on Japan, next on the United States (A–27). Of other places of origin, the leading country was the Federal Republic of Germany. These results, based on a broad definition of technology imports, are consistent with data on royalty payments to foreign countries. Of royalties paid between 1962 and 1976, about 60 percent went to Japan, 28 percent to the United States, and 5 percent to Germany (Korea 1977).

Is the heavy reliance on Japan for technology a cause for concern? Some western-educated Koreans argue in scientific and engineering circles that many Japanese technologies are modified versions of western technologies and that it would be better for Korea to import the technologies directly from western countries. Our impression, however, is that Korea has benefited more from the reliance on Japan than if it had imported technology directly from western countries. There are three reasons for this. First, the differences between Korea and Japan in factor endowments and in social and cultural structures are much less than those between Korea and western countries. Second, as Peck has characterized it, Japan is "the best of all nations in technological borrowing," in that it has shown extraordinary ability in adapting and organizing modern technology to meet the requirements of its factor endowments (1976, p. 527). Third, the nearness of Japan and the differences in factor prices between Korea and Japan make it possible for Korea to take over industries in which Japan is losing its comparative advantage, such as textiles—a point that has been made in the broader context of stages of comparative advantage (Balassa 1977). But these arguments do not mean that Korea should not diversify the countries of origin of its technology.

Technological Capability

The findings on the sources of technology show that Korean entrepreneurs were often able to unbundle the packages of foreign resources—packages consisting of technicians, machines, and manuals, as well as managers and investment capital—that characterize many transfers of technology. Because they had mastered the operation of some technology, their skills could be used in managing and operating similar technology for other products—and in importing only the additional technology they needed. Korean technological capability, augmented by information from foreign buyers and suppliers, thus supplanted licensing and direct foreign investment as means of acquiring technology. Korean firms used licensing and direct foreign investment not to replace the local effort to develop and master technology, but to start that effort. These efforts naturally broadened their capability for future efforts.[3]

Much of Korea's technology, originally foreign, was absorbed early (Westphal, Rhee, and Pursell 1981). For example, Korea in 1945 had eight cement plants with an aggregate capacity of 1.7 million tons, thirty-five factories making electrical equipment, a machinery industry producing ship engines and rolling stock, textile mills with roughly 10,000 looms and 325,000 spindles, and numerous plants producing shoes, plywood, leather goods, and other light manufactures. Much of this capacity was dismantled at the end of the Second World War, and much of what was put back into operation was destroyed during the Korean War. But what lay dormant in the reconstruction years was the experience many Koreans acquired in operating these installations—experience that bestowed on Korea a considerable capability to unbundle foreign technological packages and to select different sources of technology (Korea Economic Research Center 1961).

Consider the development of tire production, which in nearly all other developing countries has been dominated by direct investment by the major tire producers from the developed countries. The first tire plant in Korea was set up by foreigners in 1941. It was largely destroyed during the Korean War, and production did not resume until 1958. By 1962 three other plants had been established, all Korean owned. The foreign contribution to those investments is not known. But it is known that one of the producers entered no technical agreements or licensing arrangements during 1962–78 and that another embarked on a major expansion during 1969—indications of the technological self-sufficiency of those producers. Although exports (nearly all to developing countries) accounted for less than 10 percent of production in the 1960s, they increased rapidly in the 1970s, rising to 60 percent of the production of three of the firms in 1975, still primarily to other developing countries. Most of these exports were bus and truck tires, the manufacture of which is considerably more labor intensive than that of tires for passenger cars. Korea's mastery of tire-production technology is demonstrated by the $88 million turnkey plant that Daewoo completed in the Sudan in 1980, having contracted for it in 1978.[4]

Apart from the technological capability accumulated before the end of the Second World War, there probably was much learning during and after the Korean War in supplying and repairing tires for the Korean and American armed forces. Without such learning, the development of the Korean tire industry would have had to rely much more on foreign sources of investment and technology. But it was only when they embarked on the production of radial tires in the early 1970s that some of the firms found it necessary to rely on licenses, turnkey plants, and technical agreements.

An important element of all this was the policy of government for technology imports. The Korean government did not allow firms to bring in whatever technology they wanted. With typical craftiness the Koreans had a stated policy for imports of technology that was liberal but also very vague, so that discretion could reign. What came in? Technology that filled gaps, but also technology that was not bundled with a lot of excess (and expensive) baggage.[5] The government influenced the kind and amount of technology that came into the country. For infant industries, the government chose to foster them a few at a time—to foster them well and to avoid draining resources from profitable industries. Even for the infants, the government imposed discipline early on by pushing them to export. By doing all this, the government encouraged firms (and the local effort) to adapt technology and to import only what was needed. The Koreans thus were selective in the amount of technology and other baggage that came with each transfer of technology from abroad. They were also selective about the industries for which the more expensive bundled technology could be acquired through licensing and direct foreign investment: steel, shipbuilding, electronics, and some chemicals are the most important examples.

This selectivity presumably was greater because of Korea's trade regime of export promotion. Under a regime of import substitution a country wants to produce everything, not specialize. In need of technology for every industry, it cannot be fussy about what and how technology is transferred, or it must try to create technology—courses of action that are expensive, slow, or both. Usually such a country must in the early stages of industrialization rely heavily on licensing or direct foreign investment—or on R & D to supplant those foreign sources. But under a regime of export promotion a country needs to resort to licensing or direct foreign investment for fewer industries, perhaps many fewer, because it is specializing. It can also avoid heavy spending on research and on generating new technology. That is what Korea did—fill the gaps for only a few industries at a time, persistently supplanting foreign resources by domestic resources.

Many of the main industries in Korea's past industrialization—such as plywood or textiles and apparel—use technologies that can be characterized as mature, in that the mastery of well-established and conventional methods embodied in equipment readily available from foreign suppliers is enough to enable efficient production.[6] Furthermore, the products of many of these industries are either highly standardized (plywood) or differentiated in technologically minor respects (textiles and apparel). In short, for most of the industries intensively developed so far, the technology for processes and for product design has not been proprietary. So, for acquiring technology or for marketing abroad, there have been few advantages to be gained from either licensing or direct foreign investment, except in some special circumstances.

In industries for which the production technology is not product-specific, the copying of foreign products has been a means of increasing technological capability. The mechanical-engineering industries, among others, afford many examples: such processes as casting and machining, learned by producing one item, can easily be applied in producing other items. One industry that has been closely studied is textile machinery, particularly semiautomatic looms for weaving fabric (Rhee and Westphal 1977). In this, as in some other cases, Korean manufacturers have not only been able to produce a capital good that meets world standards; they have, in addition, adapted the product design to make it more appropriate to circumstances in Korea.

In other industries in which the technology is more product-specific, the mastery of underlying principles has enabled greater local participation in the technological effort associated with establishing closely allied lines of production. Thus, to facilitate the accumulation of technological capability in some industries, such as synthetic resins and fibers, the first plants were turnkey, but much smaller than either the size of the market or the size that would exhaust scale economies. Because of the rapid growth of exports and the economy, the construction of subsequent plants followed quickly, at scales much closer or equal to world scale and with Korean engineers and technicians assuming more of the tasks of project design and implementation.

By the mid-1970s Korean exporters had accumulated much more technological capability in production engineering than in plant and product engineering. The responses by firms to questions about sources for product engineering—that is, for improvements in quality, for additions to product lines, and for changes in product design, styling, and technical specifications—showed that Korean exporters, almost across the board, relied heavily on foreign sources, more so than for production engineering (A–42). In most industries, local capability was confined to production engineering and plant operation. It seldom extended to the design of products and plants, even in the many industries long established in Korea. The greater proficiency of Koreans in production engineering may be the result of a strategy to learn the easier technological tasks first and to rely on foreigners to perform the more difficult ones until such time as Koreans could devote time and effort to learn those tasks as well.

Even when production was first established to serve the local market, with exports following later, Korean firms focused their efforts on production engineering and relied on foreign sources for product engineering. The effort to master product engineering was often confined to achieving rudimentary standards. These standards may have been high enough for entering export markets, but if exports were to grow, the specifications of products sooner or later had to be tailored to the different demands of different markets. Until experience could be gained in meeting differentiated demands, exporting firms presumably found it cheaper to rely on foreign buyers for their product engineering.

The selective mixing of local capability in production and project execution with foreign capability in plant and product design—something evident in modern industries—can be seen in the development of Korea's steel industry. In slightly more than three years after the start of construction in 1970, the Pohang Steel Company began production. This construction time was roughly two-thirds that needed for similar plants in Italy and France, and less than half that needed in Brazil and India (Institute of Economic Research 1979). Korea's production-engineering capability in construction and metal-working was the main reason behind this performance. Korea's rapid learning of production technology is reflected in its consulting for other East Asian producers on operating techniques and its training of engineers for those producers. Having undergone several capacity expansions, Pohang was by 1981 the eighth largest steel producer in the free world—with a capacity of 8.5 million tons. And although the basic engineering for these expansions has been done by foreigners, the use of Korean resources has been increasing: construction work and techniques have been entirely Korean; detailed engineering work has been increasingly Korean.

The selective mixing of Korean and foreign capability is also evident in the development of Korea's shipbuilding industry. The designs for building shipyards—the Hyundai shipyard is the largest in the world—and for building ships were obtained entirely through licensing agreements (Masubuchi 1981). Koreans again focused on production engineering, such as welding processes and construction activities. But having begun construction for the Hyundai shipyard only in 1971, Korea had by 1981 carved out almost a tenth of the world market, with an annual capacity of about 4 million tons.

Conclusions

Korea in the 1960s and 1970s fostered the adoption of strategies by firms to embark on conscious technological efforts. Exporting in itself was the basis for some of this effort—through the pressure it imposes on firms for increasing efficiency. So was government policy. As a result, Korean exporting firms made an effort to close technological gaps. For some products and industries, those gaps were large, and firms found it necessary to rely initially on licensing and direct foreign investment for their technological inputs. For other industries and products, the gaps were much smaller, and firms found it necessary to rely on outside resources only for the few technological inputs they could not provide or buy in Korea. There thus appear to have been conscious efforts to be selective in importing technology and in accumulating more and more technological capability—and thereby to have local technological resources progressively supplant foreign technological resources in successive transfers of technology.

By following this course the Koreans got a lot of mileage from their investment in technology. Because they could unbundle the elements of imported technological packages, they did not waste money unnecessarily on the excessive baggage that often is a part of such packages. Nor were they kept out of production activities in which they did not possess the needed capability. They simply substituted foreign for local capability until the local capability could be developed. In shifting to more technology-intensive industries, however, Korean firms are likely to find that what worked well for traditional industries will work less well. More resources will have to be devoted to R & D to develop Korea's capabilities in plant and product engineering. More resources will have to be devoted to importing the technology for those industries. And increasingly there will have to be a strong effort to develop the full range of technological capabilities needed for a line of production.

Notes to Chapter 4

1. The method of evaluating relative importance is explained in the note to figure 4–1.

2. For the classification of modern and traditional industries, see the note to figure 4–1.

3. See Bell, Ross-Larson, and Westphal (1982) for a discussion of the accumulation of technological capability and the importance of technological efforts by firms.

4. For more on Korea's technology exports, see Westphal and others (1984).

5. Enos (1982) writes: "Summarizing the conditions of the agreements the Korean government secured with the foreign owner of the technology, the former gathered access to the most modern technique and assurance that it would be applied fully up to the limit imposed by the capacity of the equipment. Assurance was also given that its own citizens would become fully conversant with the technique and skilled in its operation and improvement" (p. 74). Shinohara (1982) describes Japan's restrictions on foreign technology until 1970, the purpose of which restrictions was to assure the acquisition of useful technology, whether from foreign or domestic sources, not to promote domestic sources.

6. The arguments here draw heavily on Westphal, Rhee, and Pursell (1981), in which some of the survey's findings on technology were first published.

5

Selectivity in Marketing

EXPORT MARKETING BY DEVELOPING COUNTRIES calls for efficient international communications by mail, telex, and telephone and efficient transport by air, sea, and land. It also calls for an efficient system of receiving foreign buyers at airports, hotels, and trade centers. And it calls for an array of producers who can meet requirements for quality and delivery. But such marketing of exports does not necessarily call for tremendous efforts by producers—or by trading companies acting on their behalf—to sell their products in the importing countries. At least at the outset. Korean firms have shown that it is possible to be successful in exporting by letting foreign buyers do much of the marketing during the early stages of export development.

There are many ways for producers to participate in the links of the export marketing chain: selecting the product, packaging it, shipping it, and in the foreign market receiving it, storing it, advertising it, and selling it to retailers, perhaps with arrangements for financing and for aftersales service. The time, risk, money, effort, and know-how required for these tasks explain why many would-be exporters simply resign themselves to producing for the domestic market. If the conditions are right, however, buyers from abroad will come in and perform as many of these tasks as are needed to start and maintain a line for export production—for a price, of course. What are the right conditions? Some important ones are low production cost, good product quality, reliable delivery, high probability of ongoing supply, and a business environment that fosters trade rather than impedes it (see Keesing forthcoming).

In this chapter we continue our analysis of Korea's success in export promotion by investigating the marketing of exports. In the first section we describe the ways Korean firms and the Korean government have courted foreign buyers to come in and perform many of the tasks of export marketing. In the second we distinguish different kinds of foreign buyers and examine their relative importance. We also explore whether firms rely on only a few such buyers for a large proportion of their sales. In the third section we describe the many tasks that foreign buyers will perform in addition to the negotiation of contracts. Where appropriate, the findings are compared with those of a later survey of sixty Korean firms exporting mainly heavy industrial products.

Courting Foreign Buyers

Before export markets can be developed, foreign buyers and Korean sellers must somehow contact each other for the first time. Once the first contact is made, there must also be some way of continuing the relationship. In Korea, several institutions develop these links.

First, the government has assisted exporting firms in their relations with foreign buyers by creating and financing the Korea Trade Promotion Corporation (KOTRA). Established in 1962, KOTRA now maintains about a hundred trade centers around the world to provide information about Korean importers and exporters, the commodities they buy and sell, and the services they need and provide in foreign investment and construction work. It has an array of publications, such as the daily *Overseas Market News*, which provides up-to-date information on trading opportunities to Korean importers and exporters, and the bimonthly *Korea Trade*, a catalog of Korean export products. KOTRA also receives foreign visitors, introducing them to Korean businessmen and government agencies, and holds trade shows throughout Korea and the world.

Second, many institutions other than KOTRA follow international market developments and assemble information for Korean exporters. Most notable among these are the Korean Traders Association and the more than thirty exporters' associations, such as the Korean Knitted Goods Exporters Association, the Korea Electronic Products Exporters Association, and the Korea Footwear Exporters Association. Most of these associations are housed, like KOTRA, at the World Trade Center in Seoul. The Korean Traders Association, though formed in 1946, did not really get under way until the export drive of the 1960s and 1970s. It now has 3,000 members. Its work ranges from acting as a collective pressure group on behalf of exporters to carrying out the functions delegated to it by government, such as issuing certificates related to trade. Besides publishing the *Korean Trade Directory* and the up-to-the-minute *Trade News Service*, the association compiles and publishes *Monthly Statistics of Foreign Trade, Statistical Yearbook of Foreign Trade, Export-Import Procedures*, and other materials related to foreign trade. All registered exporters are members of the association, contributing to its budget.

Third, some manufacturers rely on Japanese trading companies to develop their foreign markets, not only in Japan but in most of the world, including the United States. In doing this, they take advantage of the vast international network built up during the Japanese export expansion. Other firms use Korea's general trading companies, which have been encouraged by strong government policies to develop along the lines of Japan's sogo shosha.[1] The incentives for general trading companies have included preferential loans for stockpiling export commodities and higher ceilings on the foreign exchange holdings of their overseas branches. Five Korean firms were licensed as general trading companies in 1975, six more in 1976, to exploit the economies of scale in marketing, investment, and production. According to the requirements of their licenses, the general trading companies must surpass specified levels of exports and paid-in capital and operate a minimum number of branches in a minimum number of countries. These firms played a small role in Korea's export activity at the time of our survey, but by 1982 they accounted for about half of Korea's exports (see table B–8 in appendix B).

Fourth, many Korean firms have their own branches abroad. At the time of our survey most of these branches were small, typically employing only a few Korean staff and performing functions other than marketing. According to the Korea Ministry of Commerce and Industry, there were about 2,800 staff in some 1,400 branches overseas, for an average of two persons a branch, in the middle of 1979 (see table B–6 in appendix B). The findings of a 1979 survey of sixty heavy industrial firms by the Korea International Economic Institute (KIEI) show the average number of branches per company to be seven, that for general trading companies twenty-three.[2]

What was the relative importance of these various institutions in first contacting foreign customers and then maintaining relations with them? Three-fifths of the firms had direct representation by a branch or affiliated company in at least one foreign country (A–28). About a third were represented abroad by Japanese or Korean trading firms. About two-fifths relied on representation by nonaffiliated foreign companies that acted as sales agents, purchasing agents, and the like. Because a high proportion of large exporters are in the sample, the figure for firms with direct representation is higher than the average for all Korean exporters. The figure nonetheless indicates that by 1975 these exporting firms were making direct contacts with buyers in their export markets.

In all markets, representation by branches and affiliates was the most common, even though most firms had different kinds of representation in different markets (A–28). This kind of representation was most important in the United States and Canada, followed by Western Europe, Japan, the Middle East, and Asia. Many firms had more than one branch in the United States, usually an East Coast branch in New York and a West Coast branch in either Los Angeles or San Francisco. In most other countries, it was unusual for firms to have more than one branch. The low ranking of branches and affiliates in Japan, despite Japan's being the largest export market for Korea, is presumably explained by its proximity. The flight from Tokyo to Seoul takes only two hours, that from Tokyo to Pusan about an hour and a half. Interestingly, there was a lot of branch development in the Middle East, with almost all branches established after 1973. Korean exporters in the sample had only three branches in the Middle East at the end of 1973 (Korea 1974); they had twenty-three by the middle of 1976. By contrast, they had few branches in Africa, Oceania, and Latin America.

Of the exporters that used Korean or Japanese trading companies for representation in export markets, most relied solely on Japanese trading companies. (Recall that Korea's general trading companies were just getting started.) They were firms that export fish or that produce traditional textiles or synthetic fibers and textiles. It is precisely in these sectors that the Japanese have strong international marketing networks. Korean exporters apparently saw Japanese trading firms as giving access to a larger and more diverse group of foreign markets: some firms pointed out that the larger Japanese trading firms operated in many countries and in a sense represented them worldwide.

Representation abroad by foreign firms acting in other capacities— as sales agents, buyers, and so on—might range from a short-term arrangement with an importer to a long-term agreement with a foreign firm covering a wide range of responsibilities. Such representation by foreign firms was more frequent, and was thus seen to give a bigger geographical coverage, than representation by Korean or Japanese trading firms.

What did the branches, affiliates, and other representatives of

Korean firms do? They arranged market surveys and product displays, purchased raw materials, placed advertising, recruited salesmen, and participated in trade fairs (A–30). But they probably did not do much to sell products. For example, the New York branches of Korean exporting firms were small in the mid-1970s: most had two or three staff, including a typist. The largest New York branch of a Korean export firm had eight staff. A typical branch did not handle (and did not necessarily know of) all its company's exports to the United States or New York. Its main functions were displaying company products in the branch office, providing information to buyers and to the home office, making arrangements for visiting staff from Korea, arranging for market research and salesmen when asked by the home office, and arranging finance for trade both ways. One firm arranged all its market research and the hiring of salesmen through U.S. firms; other branches said that they hired Korean salesmen. Many branches were incorporated in the United States, in part because this made it easier to get credit from U.S. banks. As the KIEI survey found, however, selling and the exploration of new markets had by 1979 become the most important activities of the branches of Korean companies exporting heavy industrial products.

How did firms first contact the buyers in their new export markets? Foreign buyers, either in Korea or abroad, were mentioned two-fifths of the time (A–49). Visits to a foreign country by the firms' staff or representatives were cited about a fifth of the time. Other kinds of initial contact were mentioned much less frequently, such as discussions after trade fairs, enquiries directed through KOTRA, and enquiries directed through trade associations.[3]

More of these initial contacts, but not many more, were at the initiative of foreign concerns, not Korean. This finding is not surprising: by the mid-1970s Korea was a well-known, established exporter of a wide range of goods. There naturally were differences, not all of them significant, between the regional markets. In Japan, the EEC, and the United States and Canada—Korea's biggest markets—foreign initiative was more important, Korean less, than the average for all markets. In the other markets—smaller for Korea—Korean initiative was more important, notably in Latin America and the Middle East, but not in Oceania.

What constitutes principally foreign and principally Korean initiatives is not clear, however. For example, the initiatives for the first contacts with buyers in foreign countries—which usually means that the foreign buyer contacted the Korean exporter's overseas branch or Korean office (by mail or telex)—are principally foreign. But the foreign buyer may have been responding to initiatives that were principally Korean: the buyer may have visited a trade fair or been responding to an advertisement by the Korean exporter or to the publicity by KOTRA or a trade association. Similarly, foreign buyers may to some extent have been induced to visit Korea by such advertising and publicity.

There are many ways for a Korean firm to maintain relations with foreign buyers. For the exporting firms in the sample, periodic visits to customers and periodic visits of foreign buyers to Korea were mentioned most frequently and ranked somewhat higher than the other methods of maintaining relations with foreign buyers. Visits to customers and visits of buyers were about equally important for markets in Japan and the United States, but visits of buyers were more important than visits to customers in the EEC (A-32). Next to direct contacts (by travel to and by customers), indirect contacts by mail, through banks, and by telex and telephone were mentioned most frequently. These indirect contacts are used not only for maintaining relations with established customers, but for developing new customers. For example, many textile and garment firms mail samples to potential foreign buyers, using lists from trade associations and other sources.

The periodic visits of foreign buyers to Korea are often part of a trip to several other exporting countries, such as Singapore and Hong Kong. But many of them also maintain permanent branches or representatives in the Asian region for meeting and contracting with exporters. In 1975, 364 foreign companies had branches or representative offices in Korea. Of these, 267 were from the United States, 40 from Japan, and 36 from other countries. They included foreign banks and foreign firms with direct investments, as well as foreign trading companies, importers, and retail chains (Korea Federation of National Economic Associations 1976, pp. 756–66). Korean branches or representatives of foreign buyers were somewhat more important as a point of contact between buyers and sellers than the foreign branches and representatives of the Korean exporting firms.

In 1979 the overseas branches and offices of Korean exporters of heavy industrial products were the most important channel for maintaining regular contact with foreign buyers. The Korean branches of foreign buyers were less important than overseas travel by Korean staff and visits by buyers to Korea. So even in the heavy industries, visits by buyers to Korea and travel by Korean staff to visit buyers overseas continued to be important. And for these exporters, indirect contacts were least important (Rhee and Lee 1980).

Who the Foreign Buyers Are

Buyers of Korean exports come in many shapes and sizes. There are importers, ranging from one-man operations in Kobe, Hamburg, and Manhattan to commercial undertakings with networks of representation throughout the importing country. There are wholesalers that bypass the importers to get a better price and the importer's profit. There also are importer-wholesalers that do both. And there are retail chains and department stores, such as K-mart, Sears Roebuck, and Montgomery Ward, that buy some products in enough volume to enable them to bypass importers and wholesalers. Many large buyers in these categories have offices in Seoul. Then there are manufacturers that use Korea for the supply of such intermediate goods as steel, plywood, and cement. And there are the Japanese trading companies—Mitsui, Marubeni, Mitsubishi, and other giants with global sales networks. Added to these, among others, are the foreign branches, affiliates, and parent companies of Korean exporters and the foreign branches of Korean trading companies.

What was the relative importance to the Korean firms of this array of buyers? Firms thought of as importers were by far the most important, judging by the fact that three-fifths of the Korean respondents ranked them first (figure 5–1).[4] Wholesalers, manufacturers, Japanese trading companies, and the foreign branches or affiliates of Korean firms, were about equal in the rankings, but came much lower than importers. The relative unimportance of Japanese trading companies is of special interest because of the considerable role attributed to them in discussions in Korea and elsewhere. What is also interesting, retail chains and department stores were relatively unimportant, contrary to a fairly widespread belief that they are a major factor in developed-country imports of consumer goods from such developing countries as Korea. This result confirms the contention by Keesing (forthcoming) that retailers prefer not to expose themselves to the possibility of late deliveries and the need for warehousing inventories. In general, the findings of the KIEI survey were much the same in 1979 for exporters of heavy industrial products: importers still were most important, but overseas branches and affiliates by this time were running a strong second, ahead of wholesalers and manufacturers (Rhee and Lee 1980).

Importers were ranked first in markets in Japan, the United States, the EEC, and all other markets. Although the samples for these mar-

Figure 5-1.   *Importance of Foreign Buyers to Korean Exporters*

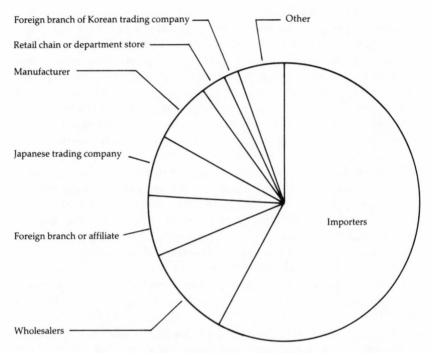

Percentage of responses indicating a source as most important

Source: A-31 in appendix A.

kets were small and not all comparisons between them were statisti-cally significant, the following differences in the rankings of other buyers are worth noting:

- Buyers that the Korean firms perceived to be mainly wholesalers were more important in the EEC and the United States than in Japan. The reason appears to be that the Japanese wholesale trade sector, unlike that in the EEC or the United States, is domi-nated by Japanese trading and importing firms.
- Retail chains and department stores were more important in the United States than in the EEC, Japan, or elsewhere, but they still had a minor role compared with U.S. importers.
- Japanese trading companies were more important as buyers for exports to Japan than for exports elsewhere.

- Orders from foreign branches (often organized as foreign sub-
  sidiary companies) of Korean trading firms were mentioned for
  Japan, the United States, the EEC and other markets, but were
  regarded as being of very minor importance.
- Manufacturers were more important as buyers in the United
  States, the EEC, and other markets than in Japan. Although
  Japanese trading companies may have been buying for their own
  or other manufacturing activities, the main explanation is probably that intermediate goods tended to be sold to manufacturers,
  and that the proportion of exports of intermediate goods to
  Japan was lower than that to other markets. Few of the newer
  exports—such as tires, machinery, steel and steel products, and
  synthetic yarns and fabrics—were exported to Japan.
- Foreign parent companies and foreign branches (including the
  foreign affiliates of Korean exporters) were about equally important in the three principal markets and the remaining markets as
  a group. Most purchases by foreign branches or affiliates, particularly in electronics, were by foreign companies with majority or
  minority holdings in the Korean exporter.

We were not able to weight these assessments of relative importance by the value of exports purchased by each type of buyer, but we
did get information on each firm's total exports and the names of
some of the largest buyers. It appears that retail chains, department
stores, and Japanese trading companies were somewhat more important than the rankings indicated alone, but importers still were the
most important by far. There nevertheless were differences between
industries, and these are roughly indicated by the following list,
which shows the categories of buyers that took more than 10 percent
of a firm's exports in 1975 (by industry):

- Textiles: importers.
- Garments: importers predominantly, but U.S. retail chains and
  department stores were very important for some large
  exporters.
- Shoes: Japanese trading companies, U.S. retail chains, and
  specialized importers.
- Plywood: U.S. plywood manufacturers.
- Electronics: foreign parent or affiliated companies, U.S. retail
  chains, and importers (for one firm).
- Tires: importers.

- Fish: Japanese trading companies and importers.
- Processed food: importers.
- Steel products: importers and manufacturers.
- Machinery: importers and manufacturers.
- Shipbuilding: shipping companies and ship-brokers.
- Tableware: importers.
- Toys, handicrafts, and sporting goods: importers.

Did the Korean exporters typically deal with just a few buyers, or did they normally have many customers who bought in smaller quantities? Two-thirds of the responding firms indicated that at least one foreign buyer normally accounted for more than 10 percent of their exports. A fifth of the firms reported that their four largest foreign buyers accounted for more than 60 percent of their exports (A–33). What is striking is that more than half the traditional textile firms did not have any foreign buyers accounting for more than 10 percent of their exports. If the textile sector is left out, more than three-quarters of the remaining traditional firms had at least some large buyers. In the modern sector, three-quarters of the firms reported that at least one foreign buyer accounted for more than 10 percent of their exports.

The concentration of foreign buyers in the exports of firms is more evident in the cumulative shares of large buyers. The incidence of high buyer-concentration, defined as a firm's having its four largest buyers account for more than 60 percent of its 1975 exports, is summarized in appendix table A–33. High buyer-concentration was greater for modern products than for traditional products, but it was greatest for resource-based products, notably fishing products, the exports of which were dominated by sales to a few large Japanese trading companies and U.S. importers. There were no textile firms with high buyer-concentration. Such buyer-concentration was particularly marked in the electronics industry. Of the four electronics firms that gave information about their buyers, two exported almost their entire output of components to their foreign parent companies; one television manufacturer sent its exports to its foreign parent company, and a second television manufacturer sent more than half its exports to a large U.S. retail chain and the rest to its foreign affiliates.

The advantage of depending on one or a few foreign buyers is that it enables the exploitation of scale economies through larger lot production, and that advantage has presumably been seen to outweigh the risk associated with such dependence.[5] In some Korean industries without obvious technical economies of scale, firms are very large. This can probably be best explained by the advantages of such firms in dealing with large foreign buyers. A good example is again the shoe industry, in which the largest firm had 17,000 employees in 1975 and sales (all exports) of about $60 million. The five shoe firms in our sample had average exports of $32 million. Similarly, two firms in the garment industry had exports of more than $30 million, one only $3 million. Many firms that were not in the sample operated successfully with annual exports of about $1 to $2 million (and few or no domestic sales).

What Foreign Buyers Do

The relations between Korean firms and the foreign buyers went far beyond the negotiation and fulfillment of contracts. Almost half the firms said they had directly benefited from the technical information foreign buyers provided: through visits to their plants by engineers or other technical staff of the foreign buyers, through visits by their engineering staff to the foreign buyers, through the provision of blueprints and specifications, through information on production techniques and on the technical specifications of competing products, and through feedback on the design, quality, and technical performance of their products by letter and telex (A–45).

Three-quarters of the firms said that the requests and recommendations of foreign buyers influenced the design, style, packaging, or technical specifications of products exported (A–42). Most of the firms confirmed that some of their exported products were made directly in accord with designs, patterns, or other specifications supplied by foreign buyers. For about a quarter of the firms in the sample, such products accounted for more than 40 percent of their exports (figure 5–2).

Did the foreign buyers mainly affect the packaging? Did they affect the design or styling (as would be expected for garments, for example)? Or did they affect the basic technical specifications? Almost three-quarters of the firms mentioned product design and styling (A–43). Packaging was also frequently mentioned, but few firms mentioned packaging alone. About half the firms indicated that requests by foreign buyers affected the technical specifications.

In a more detailed evaluation of the advantages to firms of direct contacts with foreign buyers, more than half the firms in our 1976

Figure 5-2.   *Influence of Foreign Buyers on Production*

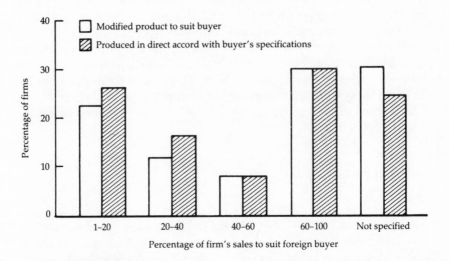

Percentage of firm's sales to suit foreign buyer

Source: Appendix table A-42.

survey considered those contacts to be important for the adaptation of product design and styling to market requirements—and for the development of new products or new product varieties (A-46). About two firms in five said that contacts with foreign buyers were important for improved techniques of quality control and for improved techniques of production; one in five, for improved cost accounting and control. Because of the activities of foreign buyers in supervising and checking export shipments, the exporting firms had a strong motive to implement effective methods of quality control.[6] Three-quarters of the firms confirmed that foreign buyers attempted some supervision over shipments, usually by preshipment inspections. Other methods included periodic visits to the factories and constant surveillance by inspectors that buyers had stationed in the factories. In addition, foreign buyers made suggestions about techniques of cost accounting and control.

It would be expected that foreign buyers would have less influence on the design, style, packaging, and technical specifications of heavy industrial exports, and the KIEI survey found this generally to be so, except for exports under licenses and joint ventures. All ship and plant exports were based on buyer specifications. And most machinery, automobiles, and electronics products exported under joint ventures followed the specification that foreign partners provided. But one electronics company exported only products of its own design, as did one automobile manufacturer. For tires, cement, fertilizer, and petrochemical products, the specifications of which are internationally standardized, the buyers had almost no influence. And for several other products, the share of exports influenced by foreign buyers was small: 10 percent for power tillers, 15 percent for farm engines, and 5 to 20 percent for home appliances. Surprisingly, most exports of steel products and iron products were based on buyer specifications, though buyers were not important in influencing the design and style of such products (Rhee and Lee 1980).

Data on advertising confirms the reluctance of Korean exporters to take over much of the marketing from foreign buyers. Two-fifths of the firms advertised in foreign markets (see table A–39 in appendix A). For most of these firms, however, the expenditure on advertising was low, and in comparison with the value of export sales it was nothing: only two firms spent more than $100,000 on advertising in export markets. Advertising was done with about equal frequency in all markets except Japan, where advertising was rare (A–37). Most advertising in foreign markets was apparently initiated by the Korean exporter: only an eighth of the firms reported that they contributed to advertising by foreign importers or distributors (A–38). The 1979 survey by the KIEI found that more than half the heavy industrial exporters advertised overseas, but for many of them this merely meant that they distributed brochures. The average advertising expenditure by the sixty firms was 0.02 percent of sales (Rhee and Lee 1980).

To promote exports, an alternative or supplement to advertising is the use of salesmen. But only an eighth of the firms had ever employed salesmen in foreign countries (A–40). Of these firms, most produced wigs, garments, and traditional textiles—one produced tires, one textile machinery. Only a few companies used salesmen before 1970, with Koreans used about as frequently as foreigners hired through sales agencies. Clearly, the use of salesmen for promoting sales in foreign markets was of minor importance; four firms in five had never used them. That this would begin to change was found by the KIEI survey, in which firms in heavy industry indicated that they planned to train or hire professional sales people. By 1979 a sixth of these firms had an overseas sales force of three or more, and this presumably included the staff of Korean branches overseas (Rhee and Lee 1980).

The use of brand names is another way of promoting exports: a

Korean brand name if Korean brand recognition is high, a foreign brand name if Korean brand recognition is low. The firms in the sample used their brand names more frequently than foreign brand names: about half the firms did not use foreign brand names at all (A–35–36). Own-brand-name products accounted for a higher proportion of domestic than of export sales, but were important in export markets nonetheless; half the firms said that own-brand-name products accounted for more than three-quarters of their exports.

The use of foreign brand names was particularly important for exports of wigs, shoes, clothing, tableware, sporting goods, and electronic products. Almost all firms in these industries exported products under foreign brand names, and for half of them such products accounted for more than three-quarters of their exports. By contrast, the use of foreign brand names was relatively uncommon for exporters in the other industries (notably in plywood, cement, textiles, machinery, and metal products). Only a fifth of the firms in these industries had foreign-brand-name exports, and these exports generally accounted for a low percentage of their total exports. The difference in the use of foreign brand names turns on the fact that most firms in the first group of industries were exporting final consumer goods.

Conclusions

The experience of Korea shows that, in the early stages of export promotion, marketing does not have to have the highest priority for many products. True, government-supported marketing initiatives are needed until private firms can develop their marketing capabilities. But in the meantime, foreign buyers will perform many if not all of the marketing tasks if prices and quality are acceptable and if deliveries are reliable. The experience of Korea also shows what is needed to attract foreign buyers and to get the export-marketing ball rolling: mainly the ability to produce an internationally competitive product, but also, and of equal or more importance, the desire to do everything needed to court those buyers. An important part of this is creating an environment in which the right incentives are determined and then granted to unleash private initiatives in production and in international competition.

Korea in the 1960s and 1970s selected ways of marketing products that initially relied heavily on foreign buyers but that apparently were gradually taken over by Korean firms. It followed this middle path of mastering marketing—learning by watching—rather than continue to rely on foreign buyers and rather than invest vast sums to set up its own elaborate marketing network at the outset. The choice enabled Korea to proceed slowly and sensibly in marketing. In addition to the decided advantage of learning marketing techniques before investing in marketing, the advantages stemming from contacts with foreign buyers—in guidance about styles, designs, and production and management techniques—were considerable. Only later, after Korean firms had learned enough from foreign buyers and become more confident about marketing, were a few large general trading companies deliberately (and selectively) encouraged by the government to take on more of the tasks of marketing. In so doing, these general trading companies have been able to exploit economies of scale in gathering information, in exploring new markets, and in establishing overseas sales networks. By 1982 these companies embraced almost 200 affiliated firms in Korea and were making half the country's exports (see table B–8 in appendix B). As Korean exports move up the technological scale, the general trading companies will be at the heart of the effort to have Korean marketing activities progressively supplant foreign marketing activities. This effort will entail much more than selling exports overseas. It will branch into gathering information, investing abroad, exporting technology, and searching for and acquiring natural resources and other inputs for the Korean industrial machine.

Notes to Chapter 5

1. For a description of Japan's general trading companies, see Young (1979).

2. The sixty firms were larger than average exporting firms and were distributed thus: ten in machinery, nine in electronics, eight in steel, eight in general trading, five each in fertilizer, automobiles, and petrochemicals, four in cement, and three each in tires and shipbuilding. The distinction between the general trading companies and the other manufacturers in the sample is blurred to the extent that both are under the same conglomerate groups. Any differences between the findings of our 1976 survey of 113 firms and the KIEI's 1979 survey of sixty firms may be attributable to the different mix of traditional-industry exporters and heavy-industry exporters and to the change in the structure of Korean export marketing between 1976 and 1979. Disentangling the two causes is of course impossible (Rhee and Lee 1980).

3. In question A–49 foreign branches of the Korean exporters were not listed as a possible source of initial contact (see the appendix). The reason is that we assumed (perhaps wrongly) that a branch would not be established in a new market in advance of initial contacts with buyers in that market. But it is possible that foreign branches

serving one market (say, the East Coast of the United States) might constitute the initial contact point with buyers in another foreign market (Latin America).

4. There obviously is some ambiguity in the responses, because all foreign buyers are importers in that they import into the country in which they operate. Some buyers may also have several functions: for example, importers often are also wholesale distributors. But discussions with personnel in the export departments of the firms lead us to believe that most respondents know the principal activities of their foreign buyers and responded accordingly.

5. See Wortzel and Wortzel (1980) for a discussion of marketing stages and the exploitation of scale economies.

6. To establish and maintain a reputation for good quality, the Korean government has administered a system for inspecting the quality of export products that might not yet be up to international standard. Started in the early 1960s, the system was inspecting the quality of about 300 export items in the late 1970s.

6

How Much of the Past Is Prologue?

Korea's exports in 1979 slumped for the first time since the country's phenomenal growth began in the early 1960s—exports that were the cornerstone of President Park Chung Hee's regime. Park was assassinated in October 1979. A wave of uncertainty followed, undermining the perceived permanence of policies that had reassured Korean businessmen for so long. In 1980 the Korean economy faltered. Real GNP was down 6.2 percent from the preceding year; real gross investment was down 24.4 percent (see table B–3 in the appendix B). And inflation was rampant. The wholesale price index was up 38.9 percent; the consumer price index, 28.7 percent.

By 1981 the Korean economy was getting back on track: real GNP was up 6.4 percent over 1980, and exports were up 17.2 percent. In 1982 Korea's GNP grew 5.4 percent, and despite the depressed trade around the world, its exports grew 4.6 percent. What had gone wrong in the preceding years? Some would argue that Korea's main problems were the same as those of other countries: higher oil prices, world recession, and increasing protectionism. Others would argue that political uncertainty was a major cause, but economic problems were surfacing before Park's assassination.

Some of Korea's economic problems of the later 1970s can be traced to the failure to plan investments in heavy industry with the usual mix of flexibility, speed, and pragmatism. Underlying this failure was the adoption of a second principal policy objective—greater self-sufficiency in meeting the country's defense needs—to be added to the first objective of export-led economic development. The new policy was implemented with greater urgency in the mid-1970s, when President Carter proposed the withdrawal of U.S. troops stationed in Korea—and, as Koreans north and south of the truce line would perceive, the corresponding withdrawal of the U.S. commitment to the defense of the South.

The effects of the government's policy to accelerate investments in heavy industries during the second half of the 1970s can be inferred from investment trends. The average annual growth of gross investments during 1977–79 was 26 percent, compared with an average of 16 percent for the entire period 1962–81. A major share of this accelerated investment was in heavy industries. Of the heavy industries, the machinery sector had the highest priority, and its share in manufacturing investment increased from less than 20 percent in 1975 to more than 30 percent (of a much greater amount) in 1979.[1] Furthermore, the increased investments in heavy industries were financed mainly by the government's preferential credit rationing. Because these investments far outstripped the country's resource capability, the investments in light manufacturing were sacrificed. In addition, export incentives were reduced, the result of the real effective exchange rate's being driven down by the high domestic inflation stemming from excessive investment and the second oil shock (Balassa 1983).

Fast becoming evident was the seriousness of duplicated investments, of excess capacity, and of the bankruptcies induced by resource constraints that prevented the completion of new plants. And even though firms and the government realized that the mistakes in heavy industry were more serious than previously imagined, the realization had come too late. Unlike other projects launched by the country's incentive policies, these could not be easily reversed or redirected, given the sheer scale of the investments. All that could be done was to try to make the best of a bad situation. In December 1978 the top economic planning minister was charged with the overriding objectives of reducing inflation and salvaging the mistakes in heavy industry. In 1980 the government forced mergers, transfers of ownership, and production specialization in such machinery subsectors as automobiles, plant equipment, diesel engines, heavy electrical equipment, and electronic communication equipment.[2] Much of the excess capacity has since been reduced in some of these sectors, but the residual effects of the misguided investments still affect other sectors.

What led to these and other mistakes in the late 1970s? For one thing, the adoption of a second principal policy objective—a competing rather than complementary objective—naturally weakened the previously singular objective of export-led economic development. The investment priority for import substitution in the heavy industries deflected attention from other sectors. Until the mid-1970s, only a few heavy industries had been promoted at a time—so that activities in other sectors would not be prejudiced and so that much could be learned from sequenced investments in successive expansions of capacity in the new industries. The establishment of the steel and shipbuilding industries are examples. Things changed in the later 1970s, however, when the government began to promote many heavy industries—and many investments in each new industry—at once. And it did this without considering the resource requirements or the constraints these would impose on the entire economy.

Second, the institutional mechanisms that linked government and business were not as effective for planning numerous investments in heavy industry as they were for designing and implementing export incentives. Until the mid-1970s the Korean style of making hasty decisions, implementing them at once, and adjusting things on the basis of observations from the real world was well suited to light industrial ventures and to policy-making for export promotion. Information from world markets could be assessed easily, as could the appropriateness of plans for future development. But that style was not well suited to a broad array of investments in heavy industry, for which the assessment of information and plans is more difficult. Unlike most large, new projects undertaken previously, the heavy industry projects had no international yardsticks for assessment. Their viability was based on unrealistically ambitious expectations about international competitiveness and exporting. And as already mentioned, even when big mistakes were discovered in heavy industry, they could not be easily remedied or abandoned because of the sheer size of the investments.[3]

Third, the manipulative institutional mechanisms, previously held in check by moderation, began to be overused, especially such informal manipulative mechanisms as the president's influencing of top businessmen. This in turn reduced informational efficiency and rendered bureaucratic planning impotent. Until the mid-1970s the carrots and sticks of manipulation had been restrained; and they achieved the desired ends. But by the mid-1970s President Park was spending more time than before with the heads of the biggest firms. This gave Park an enlarged separate forum in which to brandish his authoritarian sticks, make his nationalistic exhortations, and tantalize firms with the prospect of future rewards. In turn, the heads of firms had an enlarged separate forum in which to compete for presidential approbation. That competition had been fruitful until the mid-1970s, but it became excessive after that and turned sour in the accelerated shift to the heavy industries.

The heads of the big firms, seeking to best their competitors, began to stumble over one another in their rush to get into heavy industries. The firms involved in the shift to heavy industry were on a course that would be difficult to retreat from because of the lumpiness of the investments. Nor could they be deflected from embarking on that course. And commitments may have been informally made between the president and the corporate chairmen bypassing bureaucrats responsible for planning and investment. Moreover, it is not clear that those bureaucrats would have had the competence or determination to temper the enthusiasm surrounding the course being followed by spelling out the resource constraints of that course.

Some Basic Issues for the 1980s

One important issue for Korea is to revitalize its institutional mechanisms for economic decision-making so that they can be a continuing catalyst for export-led economic growth. The positive aspects of Korea's institutional mechanisms—so effective in carrying out the policies for export promotion—will have to be maintained and even strengthened. A step in this direction is the government's initiation of national meetings for technological development in 1982, along the lines of the monthly national trade promotion meetings. But the negative aspects of those mechanisms must be rectified, too—especially those responsible for the mistakes in heavy industry planning.

The increasing complexity of the Korean economy demands greater decentralization of economic decision-making, with more autonomy to the private sector and greater reliance on the market. At the same time, the increasing concentration of power in the hands of giant corporations demands more effective government control over monopolistic abuses of the market. Both statements have validity—at least in the context of conventional economic reasoning. But more is needed than the reasoning associated with a simple government-market dichotomy. True, if decision-making for the investments in heavy industry had relied solely on the profit motives of firms or on the central planning by the government, the mistakes might have been avoided. But such an argument ignores the basis of Korea's progress in development: collaborative efforts by the government and by Korean firms. Korea's development would not have occurred under purely private or purely public economic decision-making.[4] It has been the product of the interaction of government and business and their partnership in working toward a common goal.[5] Therefore, in the revitalization of Korea's institutional mechanisms for economic decision-making, the synergistic partnership between government and business is likely to remain important. This revitalization will take conscious efforts—to establish a system of effective checks and balances and to develop more refined ways of building a national consensus. And however much is adapted from western and Japanese systems, the final shape of those institutional mechanisms will be uniquely Korean, suited to the special needs of the Korean economy and to the temperament and historical background of the Korean people.

Along with this institutional evolution so essential for economic development come changing patterns of acquiring and mastering technology and of marketing exports overseas. The shift to newer industries that use complex technology means big changes in where and how Korean firms acquire their technology—and what they have to do to master it. In past transfers of technology, the Koreans quickly became adept at unbundling many of the packages of technology imports and at being increasingly selective in what was purchased from abroad. Korean firms, especially those in traditional sectors, have thus been able to supplant foreign resources with their own in successive investments. In the heavy industries, however, there are fewer opportunities for unbundling imported technology, and learning-by-doing will take more effort and time.

This raises questions about whether Korean firms did too little in accumulating technological capability in some activities and industries. It is not known whether the strategy of selectivity, which contributed so much to the Korean export drive, led to underinvestment in foreign technology or in R & D. What is known is that foreign technology and R & D will become much more important for Korean firms in the future—and that continuing selectivity will be needed to make the most from those investments. An important part of this will be creating an environment that can lead to optimum investments in technological development.

Added to this change in technological complexity associated with the shift to new industries is a change in the competition—and thus in marketing. For years Korea was a product taker, producing what buyers on the Asian circuit specified. In this, Korean firms generally beat the competition with prices, not with quality, and took their satisfaction in long production runs. In the newer industries, however, Korean firms are not only competing with their counterparts in Hong Kong and Singapore or with new competitors in Thailand, Malaysia, and the Philippines. They are also meeting, head on, such competitors as ITT, Siemens, and Mitsubishi. Winning in that field

will take a while. No longer breaking ahead of the pack of developing-country rivals, Korea will for a time be expending considerable
money and effort to break into the club of developed-country competitors—and to deal effectively with increases in import restrictions
placed on Korean products.

What the change in competition and the increase in import restrictions mean is that Korean firms are having to undertake much more
initiative in selling their products. The change in competition also
means that Korean firms are having to undertake more of the numerous tasks of marketing their products. This is already evident from
the high priority that heavy industrial exporters attach in their marketing strategy to training sales people and expanding their overseas
branches (Rhee and Lee 1980). The general trading companies probably will be at the heart of this effort. More than selling export commodities, they will have to diversify their activities to gathering
information, investing overseas, exporting technology, and searching
for and importing natural resources from overseas. In addition to all
this, the Koreans will, because of increasing protectionism worldwide, have to become more active in trade negotiations with foreign
firms and governments.

Lessons for Other Countries

Korea is now well along the industrial trajectory. And although
many elements of Korea's success do not or will not pertain to other
countries because of the uniqueness of those elements to Korea and
Koreans, some elements do. We conclude by spelling out some of the
more important lessons of Korea's experience for other developing
countries.

One main task in managing the entry into world markets is to
remove the disincentives to exporting. The first requirement in reducing these disincentives is to guarantee exporters free access to
imported intermediate inputs and to export financing—and to maintain a realistic exchange rate or grant additional incentives that compensate exporters for an overvalued exchange rate. The administrative arrangements for this are critical, and they naturally will differ
from country to country. Another basic requirement is smoothing the
path for exporters by providing the basic infrastructure: the ports, the
arrangements for domestic transport and communication, the zones
for export processing, and the like.

The way incentives are set and adjusted is essential in determining the right mix and level of those incentives. Instrumental in this is developing institutional mechanisms that gather and disseminate the information needed to design, implement, and maintain export incentives. Of the many institutions that make up the export bureaucracy in Korea, two have been examined here: the system of setting export targets and the practice of holding monthly trade promotion meetings. These two institutions have helped translate political resolve into bureaucratic resolve. They have also provided information needed for bureaucratic action. And they have spurred the efforts of firms to export. Without these two institutions—or something in their place—Korea's system of export promotion probably would not have been so effective, the various conventional export incentives would not have worked as well as they did, and Korea's export performance would not have been what it has been. These two institutions have, along with the rest of the institutional setup, enabled the use of some unconventional export incentives on top of the conventional incentives that make up the foundation of Korea's system of export promotion. No country should imitate the special institutional mechanisms developed in Korea, for those mechanisms must be compatible with the idiosyncratic conditions of each country. Other developing countries must consciously develop institutional mechanisms that are compatible with their society's characteristics—mechanisms that can play a catalytic role in increasing the efficiency of information flows and thus in increasing the efficiency of the incentive system.

For export incentives to be right, for the administrative arrangements guaranteeing access to those incentives to be efficient, and for the institutional mechanisms for adjusting those incentives to be effective, there must be a strong political commitment and an able bureaucracy. Underlying the effectiveness of Korea's system of export promotion has been the single-minded commitment of the country's political leadership to an outward-looking development strategy based on international competitiveness. That commitment did more than foster an efficient bureaucracy. It unified all economic agents in Korea in a common identifiable undertaking. If the Korean experience is a guide, and we think it is, the institutional setup for exporting is not going to be as effective as it might be unless there are repeated signals from the very top about the importance of international competitiveness. Not to be underestimated in all this is the importance, perhaps even the necessity, of the continuity of government. In countries where governments and policy goals change frequently or regularly, it is much tougher to convince exporters about the long-term prospects for policies that favor international competitiveness.

Another important ingredient of successful exporting is the selectivity of firms in acquiring and mastering technology. Korean exporting firms have shown that it is desirable to progressively supplant foreign technological resources by local resources. Doing this depends in large part on a country's technological base, which must be consciously developed: that Korea started with a substantial technological base points to the importance of developing such a base. Korean firms also engaged in purposive efforts to master new technology. This not only helped increase their proficiency in production. It also enabled them to rely less on foreign resources, more on their own, in successive acquisitions of additional technology. For Korea, then, licensing and direct foreign investment were relied on mainly to fill gaps in the early stages of an industry's development. For much of their technology, Korean exporting firms copied it, developed it, or turned to foreign buyers and suppliers who were happy to provide it (almost) for free. This shows that exporting can offer a direct means of improving productivity, in addition to the indirect stimulation that comes from trying to increase the penetration of overseas markets.

Korean firms have also shown that it is possible, even desirable, to be selective in the marketing of exports. Initially, and with the help of the government, they focused on fostering conditions to attract foreign buyers. In general, they let foreign buyers incur the cost of most of the tasks of marketing—in exchange for competitive prices. That way, Korean firms could gain experience by observing the mechanics of marketing and begin whittling away at some of the marketing tasks that foreign buyers performed. Most of this whittling has been by the largest firms, especially the general trading companies. But in moving up the technological scale it probably is more difficult, and more necessary, to progressively supplant foreign marketing resources by domestic resources.

The Koreans have shown, too, that there is a strong interaction between exporting and the effectiveness of a country's economic institutions, both public and private. Without effective institutions, a country may not be able to devise an effective policy for export promotion. Conversely, successful exporting appears to give economic institutions more vitality and effectiveness: an outward-looking development strategy can thus improve a country's economic institutions. Without the spur of exporting, then, it is unlikely that Korea's economic bureaucracy would have become so adept and that its institutional mechanisms would have become so effective. Nor is it likely that the management of firms would have been so effective. Other successful exporters—Japan, Hong Kong, and Singapore—have developed different institutional mechanisms. But what appears common to these countries is that the effectiveness of their economic institutions owes much to their exports—just as their exports owe much to their economic institutions.

True, these lessons do not pertain fully to all countries. It is tougher to convince would-be exporters about the longevity of policy if the government is unstable than if it is stable. It is improbable in these protectionist times that a very large economy could export as much of its GNP as Korea has. It is more difficult to keep a realistic exchange rate in a country that has substantial natural resource exports—which push for an overvalued exchange rate—than in a country that does not have such exports. And it is more difficult to marshal a national effort in countries with a heterogeneous population than in those that have a population as homogeneous as Korea's. But decision-makers in countries wildly different from Korea can still profit by studying what has been possible in Korea—and what has been achieved.

The Koreans have shown, above all, that with a strong political commitment to international competitiveness—and with effective institutions, an able bureaucracy, aggressive businessmen, disciplined workers, and the right incentives—it is possible to have world trade lead a country's economic growth and development. Such growth and development in turn benefits the country's trading partners and contributes to global trade and development. There naturally are nay-sayers who say that exporting these days is a dead end for developing countries, mainly because of growing protectionism in the developed countries. But the experience of Korea shows that it is possible to survive, indeed thrive, in world markets, if there is a clear strategy for dealing with the changing conditions in those markets. The nay-sayers ask, too, With every country trying to increase its exports, who's going to be doing the importing? Yet Korea, precisely because of its competitive edge, is and will continue to be a major importer of goods from throughout the world. Korea thus exemplifies the growth of a healthy interdependence among countries, an interdependence that can only contribute more and more to world trade and development.

Notes to Chapter 6

1. See table B–9 in appendix B.
2. See Korea Economic Planning Board (1982a,b) and Korea Federation of National Economic Associations (1982).

3. Korean planning has been characterized as indicative, with the government using industrial incentives as its main policy tool (Westphal and Adelman 1973). The planning mechanism was thus ill-equipped to deal with massive new investments in heavy industry—or to intervene between the president and the large firms.

4. See Westphal (1982a) for an elaboration of the point that as much as the market has been allowed to reign in Korea, the Korean economy has never been a paragon of free enterprise in the western sense.

5. Many recent studies have reached the same conclusion about Japan's institutional mechanisms for economic decision-making. See Vogel (1979), Magaziner and Hout (1980), and Johnson (1982).

Appendix A

The Sample, the Survey, and the Findings

OF 150 KOREAN EXPORT FIRMS surveyed in the summer of 1976, 113 returned the qualitative and quantitative questionnaires. The subjects of the qualitative questionnaire are shown in table A–i. For the analysis of the qualitative questionnaires, we classified industries and commodities in five sectors: traditional, resource-based, modern, construction, and trading companies (table A–ii). Exports of these commodities accounted for about 80 percent of the value of Korean exports in 1975. Commodity exports by firms in the sample accounted for about a third of Korea's commodity exports; contracts of construction firms in the sample accounted for a seventh of Korea's construction export contracts in 1975 (table A–iii).

On the average, these firms were much larger than the average Korean manufacturing firm; they also were larger than the average exporting firm. The mean sales of the sample firms (excluding construction) were $32 million in 1975, compared with average sales of $0.5 million for all Korean manufacturing firms (table A–iv). Similarly, the sample firms had 2,582 employees on the average, compared with fifty-seven for all of Korean manufacturing.[1]

Only sixteen of the 113 firms in the sample had some foreign equity, and of these only four had majority foreign equity. Koreans in Japan owned 100 percent of the capital of one other firm and a minority share in a Japanese-controlled firm. Japan was the main source of foreign equity, followed by the United States; the foreign holdings were concentrated in the electronics and synthetic fiber (nylon, rayon, polyester, and acrylic) industries. This relatively low incidence of direct investment by foreign firms, and the exceptions in new and technology-intensive industries, are typical of Korean industry. Also typical of Korean industry is that the capital of most firms in the sample was held by the founder of the firm or his family. In many cases the sample firms belonged to groups of firms that were related by the founder's (or his family's) ownership of the capital. These groups frequently included a trading company, meaning a company that specializes in exporting its own products and the products of group members and unrelated firms. Some groups were diversified into construction and a variety of service industries, but not into banking, which in Korea in the mid-1970s was entirely in the province of government. Twenty-three of the 113 firms in the sample had no domestic sales. Most of these were firms exporting fish, garments, silk products (shibori), and electronic components.

Note to Appendix A

1. The national data are from Korea Economic Planning Board, *Report on a 1974 Survey of Mining and Manufacturing* (Seoul 1979).

LIST OF TABLES

A–i. *Subjects of Qualitative Questionnaires*

Export Markets
   Export Markets and Foreign Trade Restrictions
   Marketing Exports
   Shipment of Exports
   Export Prices
   Sales for Exports: Intermediate Inputs
   Sales for Exports: Exported Goods
   Constraints on Growth in Major Export Markets
   Effect of the 1974–75 Recession

Domestic Markets
   Sales for Domestic Use

Incentives
   Credit
   Taxes
   Import Taxes
   Free Trade Zones
   Foreign Exchange
   Other Incentives
   Export Targets
   Monthly Trade Promotion Meetings
   General Evaluation of Incentives

Production
   Processing Fees Paid for Outside Orders
   Capacity Use
   Technology

Financial
   Machinery and Equipment

Labor
   Labor and Wages

A-ii. *Sectoral Classification of Industries and Products*

Sector, industry, and product	Number of firms
Traditional sector	45
101 Textiles	20
1 Cotton textiles	4
2 Wool textiles	1
3 Synthetic textiles	7
4 Silk and silk products	4
5 Fishing net and rope	4
102 Clothing	8
1 Clothing, not knitted	2
2 Knitted clothing (including socks)	2
3 Sweaters	2
4 Other clothing	2
103 Plywood	3
104 Shoes	6
105 Leather products	1
106 Wigs	3
107 Toys, handicrafts, and sporting goods	4
Resource-based sector	13
209 Cement	2
210 Fishing	3
211 Ginseng	1
212 Processed foods	7
Modern sector	42
313 Metal products	10
3131 Basic iron and steel	3
3132 Zinc	1
3133 Iron and steel products	6
314 Machinery	8
3141 Railway cars and parts	2
3142 Textile machinery	2
3134 Electrical equipment	3
3144 Electrical appliances	1
315 Shipbuilding	4
316 Tableware	2

317 Electronics	6
318 Tires	3
319 Sugar refining	1
320 Paper boxes	1
321 Synthetic fiber and yarns	6
322 Synthetic resins	1
Construction	4
423 Construction	4
Trading companies	9
524 Trading companies	5
525 General trading companies	4
Total	113

A–iii. *Exports by Firms in Sample, by Sector, 1975*

| | Millions of dollars | | Share of |
Export sector	Commodity exports of sample firms, 1975	Total Korean commodity exports, 1975	sample firms in total (percent)
Traditional	783	2,968	26
Resource-based	209	1,060	20
Modern	782	1,053	74
Total commodity exports	1,774	5,081	35
Value of new construction contracts	115	883	14

A–iv. *Average Size of Firms in Sample, 1975*

Export sector	Export sales	Local L/C sales	Domestic sales	Total sales	Total assets	Number of employees
			Millions of dollars			
Traditional						
Mean	13.5	3.3	4.3	21.2	20.2	2,731
Standard deviation	14.2	8.6	7.3	19.8	20.4	3,507
Number of firms	44	44	44	44	45	44
Resource-based						
Mean	11.4	0.02	13.5	24.9	36.3	1,020
Standard deviation	20.5	0.07	34.8	53.7	61.5	1,578
Number of firms	13	13	13	13	13	13
Modern						
Mean	17.1	8.0	16.9	42.0	66.1	2,918
Standard deviation	36.7	18.2	22.9	58.0	129.7	4,140
Number of firms	42	42	42	42	42	41

Construction

Mean	30.4	0.0	40.2	71.2	57.6	7,272
Standard deviation	12.3	0.0	32.7	31.6	29.2	4,522
Number of firms	4	4	4	4	4	4

Trading firms

Mean	53.0	0.0	1.5	54.5	33.3	2,582
Standard deviation	8.3	0.3	2.4	65.8	50.2	4,200
Number of firms	6	6	6	7	8	7

Total (excluding construction)

Mean	16.9	4.6	10.3	31.8	41.0	2,582
Standard deviation	25.9	13.0	20.2	46.7	87.4	3,653
Number of firms	105	105	105	106	108	105

Note: This table is based on the responses to the quantitative questionnaires. Local L/C sales (meaning sales under a "local export letter of credit") are principally sales of intermediate materials used to produce exports. But some sales of final products to Korean firms, which in turn export them, are also included.

85

Targets

Of the 113 firms in the sample, 106 returned this part of the question-naire.

A–1. *What were your export targets and actual exports in 1973–75?*

Year	Mean (millions of dollars)			Standard deviation			Number of firms	
	Target	Perform-ance	Dif-ference	Target	Perform-ance	Dif-ference	Target	Perform-ance
1973	14.1	14.2	0.6	2.2	2.0	0.6	76	86
1974	19.9	20.1	–1.8	3.0	2.8	1.3	86	96
1975	26.1	24.9	0.9	4.0	3.5	0.3	92	99

Note: Not all 106 firms replied to this question, and some for only one or two years.

A–2. *Were any of your firm's export targets for 1973–76 revised after they were originally set?*

Yes 30	No 74	No reply 2

A–3. *What is the basis for the annual export target set for your firm?*

	Number of firms
Your own estimate of what you can achieve	68
Your own estimate modified by the government	26
A formula decided by the government applied to your past export performance	8
An industrywide target agreed between your export association (or KTA) and the government, with a share allocated to your firm	7
Other (please specify)	1

Note: Ninety-six firms replied to this question, some more than once.

A-4. *When the targets were set for 1975 and 1976, how difficult did you think it would be to achieve them?*

	1975		1976	
Response	*Number of firms*	*Percentage composition of responses*	*Number of firms*	*Percentage composition of responses*
Easily surpassable without special effort	11	12	11	12
Achievable without difficulty	17	18	27	28
Requiring a special effort but no major changes in the firm's plan	47	49	46	48
Requiring a major expansion or reorganization in addition to some planned changes	10	11	10	11
Unreasonable and beyond the firm's abilities	10	11	1	1
Number of firms replying	95	100	95	100

A-5. *What methods do you use to forecast the exports your firm can achieve?*

	Number of firms
A simple extrapolation of your past export growth	43
Your share of total future exports estimated by your trade association	5
Your future capacity with allowance for the growth of domestic demand, assuming full capacity utilization	43
Your own estimate of the likely growth of demand for each of your major export products	58
Other (please specify)	6

Note: Ninety-six firms replied to this question, some more than once.

A-6. *Does your firm have any say in setting the export targets for your industry?*

Yes   59   No   42   No reply   5

The targets allocated to your own firm?

Yes   50   No   47   No reply   9

If yes, is this by:

Consultation with your export association	47
Consultation with your manufacturers' association	7
Direct consultation with the Ministry of Commerce and Industry	23
Other (please specify)	8

Note: Some of the fifty firms replying to this part of the question did so more than once.

A-7. *How much time and effort are needed to prepare and discuss export targets?*

Negligible	10
Moderate	46
Considerable	49

In an average year, what is your estimate of the man-days of time involved?

Number of man-days	Top executives	Administrative personnel
Less than 5	50	16
5–10	31	28
11–50	3	32
More than 50	3	11
Total	87	87

Note: 105 firms replied to the first part of this question, eighty-seven to the second.

A-8. *With respect to your export performance, please rank the following by the importance you attach to them.*

	Ranking by firm				
Kind of recognition	1	2	3	4	5
Recognition by the president	17	11	15	12	3
Recognition by government ministries	29	23	18	4	1
Recognition by trade or export associations	17	22	16	15	6
Publicity given to export performance	17	5	11	19	11
Pride in the firm's export performance by comparison with that of its competitors	20	17	8	10	14

Note: Not all 106 firms replied to this question, and some assigned more than one first ranking. The frequency in each cell represents the number of firms that gave the indicated rank to the kind of recognition in that row. For example, seventeen firms ranked recognition by the president first in importance, eleven firms ranked this second in importance, and so on.

A-9. *To what extent are morale and efficiency at your firm affected by your export performance and the publicity given to it?*

Influence on morale and efficiency	Administrative personnel		Export personnel		Factory workers	
	Number of firms	*Percent-age com-position*	*Number of firms*	*Percent-age com-position*	*Number of firms*	*Percent-age com-position*
None at all	9	9	4	4	13	14
Moderate	44	45	29	30	47	50
Considerable	41	42	62	63	31	33
Not applicable	3	3	3	3	3	3
Total	97	100	98	100	94	100

A–10. *What has been the effect of export targets fixed for your firm? (Check, if yes.)*

Effect	1974		1975		1976	
	Number of firms	Percentage composition	Number of firms	Percentage composition	Number of firms	Percentage composition
Contributed to a more rapid increase of production	48	42	48	32	58	37
Made no difference to the growth of production	16	14	24	16	15	10
Caused the firm to divert sales from the domestic to export markets	23	20	22	15	28	18
Reduced the profitability of the firm	8	7	17	12	14	9
Led to price-cutting, unprofitable sales conditions, and other forms of competition adverse to the firm	6	5	16	11	15	10
Led to some unprofitable exports	5	4	12	8	8	5
Raised unit costs due to the employment of inexperienced personnel or for other reasons	8	7	11	7	16	10
Led to some deterioration of product quality	1	1	2	1	1	1
Total number of responses	115	100	152	100	155	100

Note: 105 firms replied to this question, some more than once, and some only for one or two years.

A–11. *Please rank the following advantages of good export performance for your firm.*

Advantage	Number of firms			
	Ranked first	Ranked second	Ranked third	Not important
Assurance of continued government support for the firm's efforts	61	21	2	9
Greater government support for firm's efforts to develop domestic sales	4	11	21	51
Active support from the government for the firm's plans for capacity expansion	20	45	10	14

Note: Eighty-five firms replied to the question, but not for all ranks.

A–12. *If you feel that government support for your firm depends on your export performance, please check whether this government support relates to any of the following:*

Rigor of tax collection	58
Credit availability for domestic sales	7
Greater facility and speed in your dealings	38
Preferential treatment in selling to government departments or organizations	2

Note: Eighty-five firms replied to the question, some more than once.

A–13. *Has your firm or its executives obtained any special awards or recognition for outstanding export performance?*

    Yes   69   No   36   No reply   1

A–14. *Have you failed to meet any export targets during 1973–75?*

    Yes   59   No   44   No reply   3

For not meeting a target, were you penalized in any way?

    Yes   1   No   57   No reply   1

A–15. *Does your firm have any bonus schemes under which increased salaries, wages, or other incentives are related to export performance?*

    Yes   23   No   78   No reply   5

If yes, what category of personnel do these relate to?

Export sales personnel only	0
General administrative personnel only	1
Factory workers only	9
The first two categories	1
The second two categories	4
All three categories	8

Monthly Trade Promotion Meetings

Of the 113 firms in the sample, 100 returned this part of the question-naire.

A–16. *Has the president or other representative of your firm attended monthly trade promotion meetings during 1974–76?*

    Yes   42   No   48   No reply   10

If yes, indicate the number of meetings attended:

	Meetings attended (number of firms)									
Year	*0*	*1*	*2*	*3*	*4*	*5*	*6*	*7*	*8*	*9 or more*
1974	16	6	4	1	1	0	1	1	0	12
1975	5	12	4	3	1	0	1	1	0	15
1976	7	9	7	1	0	0	10	2	2	4

A–17. *Is your firm represented by your export trade association at the monthly trade meetings?*

    Yes   63   No   19   No reply   18

If yes, do you participate in discussions at your export trade association?

    Yes   37   No   23   No reply   3

A–18. *Does your export trade association regularly send a circular to your firm and to other industry members regarding the monthly trade meetings?*

    Yes   43   No   38   No reply   19

A–19. *Given your firm's experience over the past few years, please indicate to what extent, if at all, the monthly trade meetings increase the pressure to have a good export performance.*

Not at all	10
Slight or moderate increase in pressure	45
Considerable increase in pressure	30
No reply	15

A–20. *How much time and effort is needed to prepare for the monthly trade promotion meetings?*

Negligible	29
Moderate	35
Considerable	4
No reply	32

A–21. *Have the monthly trade promotion meetings significantly affected the export performance of your firm during 1974–76?*

Yes   51   No   33   No reply   16

If yes, please indicate whether your performance has been affected as a result of any of the following (rank in order of importance).

	Ranking by firm				
Results of meetings	*1*	*2*	*3*	*4*	*5*
Difficulties or delays in dealing with government ministries were resolved	21	7	3	2	1
Decisions of principle facilitated exporting	16	8	8	4	1
Industries or firms benefited from greater government support	13	12	7	1	2
In the process of preparation or at the meeting, important issues and problems were identified	12	5	6	7	1
In the process of preparation or at the meeting, important information was obtained	7	4	6	4	5

Note: Fifty-one firms replied to the second part of the question, with some assigning more than one first rank and some ranking only some of the results.

Technology

Of the 113 firms in the sample, ninety-one returned this part of the questionnaire.

A–22. *For the techniques now used for producing your main products, please indicate the importance of the following as contributions to your firm's production knowledge.*

Sources	Traditional sector	Resource-based sector	Modern sector	Construction sector	Total
		Percentage composition of rankings as important and very important			
Domestic private sources	46.0	55.5	34.2	45.8	41.2
Direct purchase or assistance	3.0	8.9	2.3	4.2	3.0
Licenses or technical agreements from Korean firms	0.0	0.0	0.5	0.0	0.2
Technical assistance from Korean parent company	2.0	2.2	1.3	4.2	1.8
Technical assistance from Korean joint-venture partners	1.0	6.7	0.5	0.0	1.0
Technology embodied in Korean labor and management	33.2	42.2	24.2	25.0	29.4
Technical staff who previously worked with other Korean producers	12.2	13.3	8.8	4.2	10.5
Local technical know-how	21.0	28.9	15.4	20.8	18.9
Korean suppliers of capital equipment or raw materials	6.6	2.2	2.9	8.3	4.8
Korean buyers	3.2	2.2	4.8	8.3	4.0

Foreign private sources	48.9	54.0	54.4	40.0	44.6
Direct purchase or assistance	16.0	16.6	21.0	11.1	12.0
Licenses or technical agreements from foreign firms	8.4	8.3	12.5	6.7	4.9
Technical assistance from foreign companies	5.0	8.3	5.1	2.2	5.1
Technical assistance from foreign joint-venture partners	2.6	0.0	3.4	2.2	2.0
Foreign technology embodied in Korean labor and management (technical staff with experience in foreign factories)	13.2	8.3	18.6	8.9	9.0
Foreign suppliers of capital equipment or raw materials	10.7	20.8	8.2	11.1	12.4
Foreign buyers	9.0	8.3	6.6	8.9	11.2
Government-supported R&D or information sources	9.0	0.0	9.8	4.4	9.2
Technical assistance from the Korean Institute of Science and Technology	4.6	0.0	5.3	0.0	4.6
Technical information from the Korean Science and Technology Information Center	4.4	0.0	4.5	4.4	4.6
Other sources	1.0	0.0	1.6	0.0	0.2
Total	100.0	100.0	100.0	100.0	100.0
Aggregate frequencies	856	24	377	45	410
Number of products or processes	241	6	96	23	116
Number of firms responding	88	3	36	8	41

A–22–1. Sources of Technology: Traditional Export Sector

								Percentage composition of rankings as important and very important
Sources	Textiles	Clothing	Plywood	Shoes	Leather products	Wigs	Toys, handicrafts, and sporting goods	Total
Domestic private sources	46.9	44.9	50.0	52.2	36.4	40.0	20.0	46.0
Direct purchase or assistance	4.4	1.8	0.0	0.0	0.0	0.0	0.0	3.0
Licenses or technical agreements from Korean firms	0.0	0.0	0.0	0.0	0.0	0.0	0.0	0.0
Technical assistance from Korean parent company	3.4	0.9	0.0	0.0	0.0	0.0	0.0	2.0
Technical assistance from Korean joint-venture partners	1.0	0.9	0.0	0.0	0.0	0.0	0.0	1.0
Technology embodied in Korean labor and management	32.7	31.0	50.0	38.6	36.4	40.0	20.0	33.2
Technical staff who previously worked with other Korean producers	12.7	10.3	7.1	22.7	0.0	20.0	0.0	12.2
Local technical know-how	20.0	20.7	42.9	15.9	36.4	20.0	20.0	21.0
Korean suppliers of capital equipment or raw materials	5.9	7.8	0.0	13.6	0.0	0.0	0.0	6.6
Korean buyers	3.9	4.3	0.0	0.0	0.0	0.0	0.0	3.2

Foreign private sources	43.2	39.7	42.9	45.5	63.6	60.0	79.9	44.6
Direct purchase or assistance	12.7	11.3	0.0	13.7	0.0	20.0	20.0	12.0
Licenses or technical agreements from foreign firms	4.9	5.2	0.0	2.3	0.0	20.0	13.3	4.9
Technical assistance from foreign companies	4.9	5.2	0.0	11.4	0.0	0.0	0.0	5.1
Technical assistance from foreign joint-venture partners	2.9	0.9	0.0	0.0	0.0	0.0	6.7	2.0
Foreign technology embodied in Korean labor and management (technical staff with experience in foreign factories)	10.2	6.0	0.0	13.6	9.0	0.0	13.3	9.0
Foreign suppliers of capital equipment or raw materials	11.7	7.7	42.9	13.6	18.2	40.0	13.3	12.4
Foreign buyers	8.8	14.7	0.0	4.6	36.4	0.0	33.3	11.2
Government-supported R&D or information sources	8.8	15.4	7.1	2.3	0.0	0.0	0.0	9.2
Technical assistance from the Korean Institute of Science and Technology	3.9	7.7	7.1	2.3	0.0	0.0	0.0	4.6
Technical information from the Korean Science and Technology Information Center	4.9	7.7	0.0	0.0	0.0	0.0	0.0	4.6
Other sources	0.0	0.0	0.0	0.0	0.0	0.0	0.0	0.0
Total	*100.0*	*100.0*	*100.0*	*100.0*	*100.0*	*100.0*	*100.0*	*100.0*
Aggregate frequencies	205	116	14	44	11	5	15	410
Number of products or processes	56	30	6	11	4	3	6	116
Number of firms responding	20	7	3	5	1	2	3	41

A–22–2. *Sources of Technology: Resource-based Export Sector*

Sources	Percentage composition of rankings as important and very important			
	Cement	Fishing	Processed food	Total
Domestic private sources	42.9	50.0	58.4	55.5
Direct purchase or assistance	0.0	0.0	11.1	8.9
Licenses or technical agreements from Korean firms	0.0	0.0	0.0	0.0
Technical assistance from Korean parent company	0.0	0.0	2.8	2.2
Technical assistance from Korean joint-venture partners	0.0	0.0	8.3	6.7
Technology embodied in Korean labor and management	42.9	50.0	41.7	42.2
Technical staff who previously worked with other Korean producers	0.0	0.0	16.7	13.3
Local technical know-how	42.9	50.0	25.0	28.9
Korean suppliers of capital equipment or raw materials	0.0	0.0	2.8	2.2
Korean buyers	0.0	0.0	2.8	2.2

Foreign private sources	57.1	50.0	36.1	40.0
Direct purchase or assistance	0.0	0.0	13.9	11.1
Licenses or technical agreements from foreign firms	0.0	0.0	8.3	6.7
Technical assistance from foreign companies	0.0	0.0	2.8	2.2
Technical assistance from foreign joint-venture partners	0.0	0.0	2.8	2.2
Foreign technology embodied in Korean labor and management (technical staff with experience in foreign factories)	28.5	0.0	5.6	8.9
Foreign suppliers of capital equipment or raw materials	28.6	0.0	8.3	11.1
Foreign buyers	0.0	50.0	8.3	8.9
Government-supported R&D or information sources	0.0	0.0	5.5	4.4
Technical assistance from the Korean Institute of Science and Technology	0.0	0.0	0.0	0.0
Technical information from the Korean Science and Technology Information Center	0.0	0.0	5.5	4.4
Other sources	0.0	0.0	0.0	0.0
Total	100.0	100.0	100.0	100.0
Aggregate frequencies	7	2	36	45
Number of products or processes	3	2	18	23
Number of firms responding	2	2	4	8

A-22-3. Sources of Technology: Modern Export Sector

Percentage composition of rankings as important and very important

Sources	Metal	Machinery	Ship-building	Table-ware	Electronics	Tires	Sugar refinery	Synthetic fiber and resin	Total
Domestic private sources	39.9	33.3	39.7	41.2	30.0	8.3	28.6	29.5	34.2
Direct purchase or assistance	3.3	0.0	8.4	0.0	0.0	0.0	0.0	0.0	2.3
Licenses or technical agreements from Korean firms	0.0	0.0	2.4	0.0	0.0	0.0	0.0	0.0	0.5
Technical assistance from Korean parent company	3.3	0.0	3.6	0.0	0.0	0.0	0.0	0.0	1.3
Technical assistance from Korean joint-venture partners	0.0	0.0	2.4	0.0	0.0	0.0	0.0	0.0	0.5
Technology embodied in Korean labor and management	26.6	26.2	19.3	41.2	22.9	8.3	28.6	25.0	24.2
Technical staff who previously worked with other Korean producers	13.3	9.5	7.2	5.9	8.6	0.0	14.3	6.8	8.8
Local technical know-how	13.3	16.7	12.1	35.3	14.3	8.3	14.3	18.2	15.4
Korean suppliers of capital equipment or raw materials	5.0	1.2	2.4	0.0	7.1	0.0	0.0	0.0	2.9
Korean buyers	5.0	5.9	9.6	0.0	0.0	0.0	0.0	4.5	4.8
Foreign private sources	38.4	59.5	45.8	52.9	60.0	83.2	57.2	65.8	54.4
Direct purchase or assistance	8.4	19.1	21.6	5.9	30.0	49.9	28.6	22.7	21.0

Licenses or technical agreements from foreign firms	6.7	19.1	10.8	0.0	10.0	33.3	14.3	13.6	12.5
Technical assistance from foreign companies	1.7	0.0	10.8	0.0	10.0	8.3	14.3	0.0	5.1
Technical assistance from foreign joint-venture partners	0.0	0.0	0.0	5.9	10.0	8.3	0.0	9.1	3.4
Foreign technology embodied in Korean labor and management (technical staff with experience in foreign factories)	18.3	25.0	12.1	17.6	18.5	33.3	14.3	15.9	18.6
Foreign suppliers of capital equipment or raw materials	10.0	9.5	2.4	11.8	8.6	0.0	14.3	13.6	8.2
Foreign buyers	1.7	5.9	9.7	17.6	2.9	0.0	0.0	13.6	6.6
Government-supported R&D or information sources	*21.7*	*7.2*	*14.5*	*0.0*	*2.9*	*8.3*	*14.2*	*4.6*	*9.8*
Technical assistance from the Korean Institute of Science and Technology	10.0	4.8	7.2	0.0	2.9	8.3	0.0	2.3	5.3
Technical information from the Korean Science and Technology Information Center	11.7	2.4	7.3	0.0	0.0	0.0	14.2	2.3	4.5
Other sources	*0.0*	*0.0*	*0.0*	*5.9*	*7.1*	*0.0*	*0.0*	*0.0*	*1.6*
Total	*100.0*	*100.0*	*100.0*	*100.0*	*100.0*	*100.0*	*100.0*	*100.0*	*100.0*
Aggregate frequencies	60	84	83	17	70	12	7	44	377
Number of products or processes	17	23	13	6	19	4	1	13	96
Number of firms responding	8	6	4	1	5	3	1	8	36

A-22-4. *Sources of Technology: Construction Export Sector*

Sources	Percentage composition of rankings as important and very important
Domestic private sources	
Direct purchase or assistance	45.8
Licenses or technical agreements from Korean firms	4.2
Technical assistance from Korean parent company	0.0
Technical assistance from Korean joint-venture partners	4.2
Technology embodied in Korean labor and management	0.0
Technical staff who previously worked with other Korean producers	25.0
Local technical know-how	4.2
	20.8
Korean suppliers of capital equipment or raw materials	8.3
Korean buyers	8.3
Foreign private sources	
Direct purchase or assistance	54.0
	16.6

Licenses or technical agreements from foreign firms	8.3
Technical assistance from foreign companies	8.3
Technical assistance from foreign joint-venture partners	0.0
Foreign technology embodied in Korean labor and management (technical staff with experience in foreign factories)	8.3
Foreign suppliers of capital equipment or raw materials	20.8
Foreign buyers	8.3
Government-supported R&D or information sources	
Technical assistance from the Korean Institute of Science and Technology	0.0
Technical information from the Korean Science and Technology Information Center	0.0
Other sources	0.0
Total	*100.0*
Aggregate frequencies	24
Number of products or processes	6
Number of firms responding	3

A-23. *For product design, were any of your products first developed by modifying foreign originals?*

Yes   30   No   43   No reply   18

Export sector and industry	Number of firms that answered the questionnaire	Number of firms that modified foreign originals	Firms modifying as a percentage of firms answering	Number of products modified
Traditional	41	13	32	23
Textiles	20	5	25	5
Clothing	7	1	14	2
Plywood	3	1	33	1
Shoes	5	4	80	12
Leather	1	0	0	—
Wigs	2	1	50	1
Toys	3	1	33	2
Resource-based	8	2	5	7
Processed food	4	2	50	7
Cement	2	0	0	—
Fishing	2	0	0	—
Modern	36	13	36	28
Metal products	8	1	13	5
Machinery	6	6	100	13
Shipbuilding	4	1	25	1
Electronics	5	3	60	6
Tableware	1	0	0	—
Tires	3	2	67	3
Sugar refinery	1	0	0	—
Synthetic fiber and yarn	8	0	0	—
Trading companies	3	2	67	2
Trading companies	1	1	100	1
General trading companies	2	1	50	1
Total	88	30	34	60

— Zero or data not available.

Note: The three construction firms are excluded.

A–24. *Have you obtained or applied for patents for products or processes developed by your firm?*

Yes   21   No   61   No reply   9

Export sector and industry	Number of firms that answered the questionnaire	Number of firms that obtained or applied for patents	Firms obtaining or applying as percentage of firms answering
Traditional	41	13	32
Textiles	20	4	20
Clothing	7	1	14
Plywood	3	1	33
Shoes	5	4	80
Leather	1	0	0
Wigs	2	2	100
Toys and sporting goods	3	1	33
Resource-based	8	2	25
Processed food	4	1	25
Cement	2	1	50
Fishing	2	0	0
Modern	36	6	17
Metal products	8	2	25
Machinery	6	1	17
Shipbuilding	4	0	0
Electronics	5	1	20
Tableware	1	0	0
Tires	3	1	33
Sugar refinery	1	0	0
Synthetic fiber and yarn	8	1	13
Construction	3	0	0
Trading companies	3	0	0
Trading companies	1	0	0
General trading companies	2	0	0
Total	91	21	23

A–25. *For major items of new technology acquired in the past four or five years, please indicate the approximate time your staff needed to become fully familiar and competent in its use. (For technology recently acquired, please give your estimate of the likely time.)*

Export sector and industry	Firms that replied to the question	Number of representative technologies	Learning periods (years)		Number of observations
			Mean	Standard deviation	
Traditional	13	23	1.3	1.0	23
Textiles	8	16	1.4	1.1	16
Clothing	3	4	1.0	1.4	4
Leather	1	2	1.3	0.4	2
Toys	1	1	1.0	0.0	1
Resource-based					
Processed food	2	3	0.4	0.5	3
Modern	17	42	3.2	2.5	41
Metal products	3	8	3.1	3.2	8
Machinery	4	12	2.6	2.1	12
Shipbuilding	2	6	5.0	1.9	6
Tableware	1	2	1.3	1.1	2
Electronics	2	7	4.1	3.2	7
Tires	2	4	2.2	2.5	3
Synthetic fiber and yarn	3	3	2.0	1.0	3
Construction	2	5	2.2	1.0	5
General trading companies	1	1	1.3	0.0	1
Total	35	74			73

A-26. *Was your firm the first to introduce any production technologies in Korea?*

Yes   33   No   36   No reply   22

If yes, please provide the following information:

Export sector and industry	Number of firms responding	Number of firms that were first	Firms first, as a percentage of firms responding	Number of technologies
Traditional	41	12	29	15
Textiles	20	7	35	9
Clothing	7	2	29	2
Plywood	3	0	0	—
Shoes	5	1	20	1
Leather	1	1	100	1
Wigs	2	0	0	—
Toys	3	1	33	2
Resource-based	8	3	38	4
Cement	2	2	100	2
Fishing	2	0	0	—
Processed food	4	1	25	2
Modern	36	18	50	26
Metal products	8	4	50	6
Machinery	6	4	67	10
Shipbuilding	4	2	50	3
Tableware	1	1	100	2
Electronics	5	0	0	0
Sugar refinery	1	0	0	—
Tires	3	3	100	2
Synthetic fiber and yarn	8	4	50	3
Construction	3	1	33	3
Trading companies	3	1	33	3
Trading companies	1	0	0	0
General trading companies	2	1	50	0
Total	91	35	38	51

— Zero or data not available.

A-27. *Please rank the importance of the following foreign sources of your firm's technical production knowledge:*

Country	Firms ranking the country first	Firms ranking the country second	Firms ranking the country third	Firms ranking the country fourth
Japan	61	15	5	0
United States	18	33	10	1
West Germany	1	15	18	3
Others	2	4	3	6

Note: Eighty-two firms replied to the question, but not for all countries.

Marketing

Of the 113 firms in the sample, ninety-five returned this part of the questionnaire.

A-28. *Apart from normal banking contracts, what representation do you maintain in foreign markets?*

	Number of firms			
	Branches or affiliated companies	Japanese trading companies	Korean trading companies	Foreign companies as sales agents or representatives
Represented in at least one foreign country by	57	22	11	36
Giving representation by country	48	15	6	25
Represented in:				
United States and Canada	47	3	3	8
Japan	27	3	1	8
Asia and Southeast Asia (excluding Japan)	22	12	5	24
Middle East	23	3	—	10
Africa	7	1	—	1
Oceania	4	1	—	2
European Economic Community	32	8	—	14
Other Europe	3	1	—	5
Central and Latin America	12	2	—	—
All markets	177	34	9	72

— Zero or data not available.

Note: Responses to "other means of representation" were disregarded when they referred to representation by KOTRA, foreign importers, Korean embassies, and so on. We have assumed this to mean that the firms were not directly represented.

A–29. *How are your foreign representatives remunerated?*

	Foreign branches or affiliates	Other representatives
Commission on export sales	6	2
General business commission	1	1
Annual payment	40	13
Other (please specify)	3	1

A–30. *Please indicate whether your representatives abroad undertake any of the following activities on behalf of your firm.*

	Foreign branches or affiliates		Other representatives	
Activities	Frequency	Percentage of fifty-five firms replying	Frequency	Percentage of seventeen firms replying
Recruiting salesmen	16	29.1	3	17.7
Advertising	21	38.2	2	11.8
Dealing with returns of defective merchandise	7	12.7	2	11.8
Purchasing materials or equipment for import to your firm in Korea	22	40.0	7	41.2
Arranging displays of your products	26	47.3	7	41.2
Arranging participation in trade fairs	11	20.0	9	52.9
Arranging market surveys for your firm's products	39	70.9	14	82.4
Other	3	5.5	1	5.9

Note: Fifty-eight firms replied, fifty-five about foreign branches and affiliates, seventeen about other representatives. Some indicated more than one activity.

A-31. Please indicate the relative importance of the following types of buyer in each of your principal export markets and in your other export markets.

Type of buyer	Percentage frequencies of ranks						Unimportant or not applicable	Sum of rows
	1	2	3	4	5	6-9		
	For forty-one firms that distinguished their principal export markets[a]							
Importers	61.0	12.1	0.4	1.4	—	0.7		75.6
Wholesalers	6.4	11.4	9.9	5.0	2.1	1.4		36.2
Retail chains and department stores	0.7	0.7	6.4	7.1	1.4	0.7		17.0
Manufacturers	7.8	14.2	5.0	3.6	1.4	—		32.0
Foreign parent company	1.4	—	—	—	—	—		1.4
Foreign branches or affiliates	8.5	4.3	8.5	3.6	2.8	—		27.7
Foreign branches of Korean trading companies	2.8	2.8	1.4	8.5	0.7	—		16.2
Japanese trading companies	6.4	9.2	1.4	2.1	2.8	—		21.9
Other	5.0	—	1.4	—	—	—		6.4
	100.0							

For thirty-nine firms that did not distinguish their principal export markets [b]

Importers	66.7	18.0	2.6	5.1	—	—	7.7	100.0
Wholesalers	20.1	23.1	12.8	5.1	—	—	38.5	100.0
Retail chains and department stores	5.1	5.1	7.7	12.8	—	—	69.2	100.0
Manufacturers	5.1	18.0	12.8	10.3	—	—	53.9	100.0
Foreign parent company	2.6	—	—	—	—	—	97.4	100.0
Foreign branches or affiliates	7.7	18.0	5.1	5.1	—	—	64.1	100.0
Foreign branches of Korean trading companies	—	—	5.1	5.1	—	—	89.7	100.0
Japanese trading companies	10.3	12.8	5.1	5.1	2.6	—	64.1	100.0
Other	2.6	—	—	5.1	—	—	92.3	100.0

— Zero or data not available.

a. The frequencies are expressed as percentages of the 141 first rankings (including a small number of ties): importers were ranked second seventeen times, or 12.1 percent of the 141 first rankings. The sum of each row indicates the frequency with which the particular type of buyer was mentioned and given a rank.

b. These firms provided rankings of the overall importance of the different buyers in all their principal export markets. The frequencies show the percentage of the thirty-nine firms indicating each rank.

A-32. Please indicate the relative importance of the following methods of contacting and maintaining relations with foreign buyers in each export markets.

Type of contact	Percentage frequencies of ranks						Unimportant or not applicable	Sum of rows
	1	2	3	4	5	6-9		
	For thirty-four firms that gave separate rankings[a]							
Periodic visits to customers	19.8	26.4	11.3	8.5	—	—		66.0
Affiliates, subsidiaries, or branches of your company abroad	17.9	12.3	5.7	0.9	0.9	—		37.7
Periodic visits of foreign buyers to Korea	12.3	17.0	25.5	8.5	0.9	—		64.2
Foreign buyers or their representatives stationed in Korea	17.0	9.4	5.7	7.6	0.9	0.9		41.5
Indirect contacts only (mail, banks, and so on)	24.5	6.6	7.6	10.4	3.8	0.9		53.8
Other	8.5	2.8	2.8	—	—	—		14.1
	100.0							

For forty-four firms that gave overall rankings [b]

Periodic visits to customers	22.7	29.6	11.4	9.1	2.3	—	22.7	100.0
Affiliates, subsidiaries, or branches of your company abroad	22.7	11.4	2.3	6.8	—	—	56.8	100.0
Periodic visits of foreign buyers to Korea	27.3	34.1	13.6	6.8	—	—	18.2	100.0
Foreign buyers or their representatives stationed in Korea	15.9	11.4	15.9	6.8	—	—	50.0	100.0
Indirect contacts only (mail, banks, and so on)	15.9	13.6	15.9	18.2	—	—	36.4	100.0
Other	4.6	2.3	—	2.3	—	—	90.9	100.0

— Zero or data not available.

a. In all there were 106 first rankings (including a small number of ties). The frequencies are expressed as percentages of 106. "Periodic visits to customers" were ranked second 28 times, or 26.4 percent of the number of first rankings.

b. The frequencies show the percentages of the forty-nine firms indicating each particular rank.

A–33. Do any individual foreign buyers normally account for more than 10 percent of your total export sales?

Yes 62   No 28

If yes, please indicate the approximate percentage share of your total export sales in 1975 accounted for by such buyers.

Export sector and industry	Number of firms responding	Number of firms with large foreign buyers (buyers accounting for more than 10 percent of exports)	Number of firms for which information on large buyers available	Number of firms indicating that first four large foreign buyers accounted for more than 60 percent of exports in 1975
Traditional sector	44	28	25	4
Textiles	21	10	8	0
Clothing	8	5	4	2
Plywood	3	3	3	0
Shoes	5	4	4	1
Leather	1	1	1	0
Wigs	3	3	3	1
Toys, handicrafts, and sporting goods	3	2	2	0

Resource-based sector	11	9	8	6
Cement	2	1	1	1
Fishing	4	4	4	3
Ginseng	1	1	1	1
Processed food	4	3	2	1
Modern sector	32	24	19	7
Metal products	9	8	5	0
Machinery	8	5	4	2
Tableware	3	1	1	0
Electronics	5	5	4	4
Tires	2	2	2	0
Sugar refining	1	1	1	1
Synthetic fiber and yarn	4	2	2	0
Trading companies	3	1	0	0
Trading companies	1	0	0	0
General trading companies	2	1	0	0
Total	90	62	52	17

A–34. *Are you exporting under long-term contracts?*

Yes   32

Regions mentioned with respect to forty contracts were:

United States and Canada	17
Middle East	10
Japan	6
Other Asia	4
European Economic Community	2
Oceania	1
	40

For thirty-one of these contracts, the firms gave the contract periods, distributed as follows:

Months	Number of contracts	Percentage composition of contracts
1–6	9	29.0
7–12	15	48.4
13–24	3	9.7
24–26	4	12.9
Total	31	100.0

A–35. *Are some or all of your products sold using your own brand name?*

Yes   68   No   25   No reply   2

If yes, please indicate the approximate percentage of your brand name products in your total sales.

Own brand name sales	Domestic market		Export markets	
	Number of firms	Percentage composition	Number of firms	Percentage composition
100 percent	41	67.2	26	38.2
75–99 percent	3	4.9	17	25.0
25–75 percent	1	1.6	11	16.2
10–25 percent	1	1.6	5	7.4
Less than 10 percent	2	3.3	7	10.3
Zero	1	1.6	1	1.5
No answer	12	19.7	1	1.5
Total	61	100.0	68	100.0

Note: Sixty-eight firms indicated that at least some products were sold under their own brand name, but seven did not have any domestic sales and are not included in the sample of sixty-one firms for the domestic market.

A–36. *Are some of your products sold using foreign brand names?*

Yes   31   No   40   No reply   5

If yes, please indicate the approximate percentage of foreign brand name products in your total sales.

	Domestic market		Export markets	
Foreign brand name sales	Number of firms	Percentage composition	Number of firms	Percentage composition
100 percent	0	0.0	8	25.8
75–99 percent	0	0.0	10	32.3
25–75 percent	1	5.3	7	22.6
10–25 percent	1	5.3	4	12.9
Less than 10 percent	1	5.3	2	6.5
Zero	0	0.0	0	0.0
No answer	16	84.2	0	0.0
Total	19	100.0	31	100.0

Note: Thirty-one firms indicated that at least some of their products were sold under foreign brand names, but twelve did not have any domestic sales and are excluded from the sample of nineteen firms for the domestic market.

A–37. *Do you advertise in your principal foreign markets?*

Yes   38   No   57

If yes, in what markets?

Market	Number of the twenty-six (of thirty-eight) firms that said they advertised and that specified markets
United States and Canada	13
Japan	2
Other Asia	9
Middle East	10
Africa	0
Oceania	1
European Economic Community	13
Other Europe	0
Central and Latin America	0

A–38. *Do you contribute to the cost of advertisements made for your product by foreign importers and distributors?*

Yes   12   No   72   No reply   11

A–39. *Please give your advertising expenditure for 1975 in domestic and foreign markets.*

Advertising expenditure (million won)	Domestic market		Export markets	
	Number of firms	Percentage composition	Number of firms	Percentage composition
No reply or zero	45	58.4	65	68.4
1–10	12	15.6	19	20.0
11–50	3	3.9	9	9.4
51–100	5	6.5	1	1.1
101–500	11	14.3	1	1.1
More than 500	1	1.3	0	0.0
Total	77	100.0	95	100.0

Note: Eighteen of the ninety-five firms had no domestic sales. The eight firms that did not respond about their expenditure on export advertising indicated that they did advertise in foreign markets.

A–40. *Have you ever employed salesmen to promote your products in foreign countries?*

    Yes   12   No   78   No reply   5

Were the salesmen:

    Koreans employed by your own firm?   8
    Foreigners hired through sales agencies?   9
    Other?   2

A–41. *Is aftersales service essential for promoting the sales of any of your products?*

    Yes   23   No   68   No reply   4

In your export markets, is this aftersales service provided by:

    Foreign importers?   11
    Foreign branches or affiliates of your firm?   7
    Foreign branches of Korean trading firms?   1
    Other methods? (please explain)   8

A–42. *Are you influenced by requests and recommendations by foreign buyers for technical specifications, design, style, or packaging of your exports?*

Yes   68   No   13   No reply   14

If yes, approximately what percentage of your exports are:

Modified to suit the requests of individual foreign buyers?
Produced directly in accord with designs, patterns, and the like
   supplied by foreign buyers?

What percentage (if any) of your domestic sales are:

Modified to suit the requests of individual foreign buyers?
Produced directly in accord with designs, patterns, and the like
   supplied by foreign buyers?

Percentage of exports or domestic sales	Exports and foreign buyers		Domestic sales and domestic buyers	
	Modified	Buyers' designs, patterns, and so on	Modified	Buyers' designs, patterns, and so on
	Number of firms			
1–10	11	6	7	4
11–20	4	12	2	1
21–40	8	10	7	1
41–60	4	4	0	1
61–80	8	6	0	0
81–100	12	14	3	2
Subtotal	47	52	19	9
Influenced, but no details	20	16	6	5
Total	67	68	25	14

Note: Eleven firms indicated that 1–10 percent of their exports were "modified" to suit the requests of individual foreign buyers; six, that 1–10 percent of their exports were "produced directly" in accord with designs, patterns, and the like supplied by foreign buyers.

A–43. *What did these requests by foreign buyers affect?*

Area	Number of firms	Percentage of sixty-five firms replying
Basic technical specifications	18	27.7
Minor aspects of technical specifications	15	23.1
Product design and styling	47	72.3
Packaging	25	38.5

Note: Some firms identified more than one area.

A–44. *How do foreign buyers attempt to supervise your export shipments?*

Method of supervision	Number of firms	Percentage of seventy firms replying	Percentage of ninety-five firms in sample
Periodic visits to factory	18	25.7	19.0
Stationing inspectors in factory	6	8.6	6.3
Inspections before shipment in Korea	41	58.6	43.2
Other methods	17	24.3	17.9

Note: Some firms identified more than one method.

A–45. *Has your firm directly benefited from technical information that foreign buyers provide?*

Yes   42   No   44   No reply   9

If yes, in what ways?

Thirty-seven of the forty-two firms that said "yes" gave some indication of how they benefited: seventeen mentioned visits to their plants by engineers or other technical staff of the foreign buyers; two mentioned exchange visits of their own engineering staff to the foreign buyers. Also mentioned were a variety of other benefits: the provision of blueprints, specifications, information on production techniques, and feedback on the design, quality, or technical performance of their products by letter and telex.

A–46. *Please evaluate the importance to your firm of the following possible advantages of direct contacts with foreign buyers (if any):*

Advantages to the firm	Percentage of firms replying					
	Very important	Important	Of minor importance	Unimportant or not applicable	No reply	Total
Improved production techniques	12.6	26.3	23.2	22.1	15.8	100.0
Better adaptation of product design and styling to market requirements	30.5	31.6	11.6	15.8	10.5	100.0
The development of new products or new product varieties	26.3	30.5	20.0	10.5	12.6	100.0
Improved quality control techniques	11.6	27.3	24.2	17.9	19.0	100.0
Improved cost accounting and cost control	6.3	14.7	17.9	40.0	21.1	100.0
Other	0.0	1.1	1.1	9.5	88.4	100.0

129

A–47. *Please evaluate the following as sources of information for style changes, for improvements to the quality of existing products, and for additions to your product line.*

	Percentage of eighty-seven firms replying				
Source of information	Important	Of minor importance	Unimportant or not applicable	No evaluation	Total
Your own domestic sales staff	25.3	23.0	27.6	24.1	100.0
Domestic buyers	25.3	26.4	26.4	21.9	100.0
Foreign buyers with whom you have direct contacts	71.3	17.2	11.5	0.0	100.0
Foreign buyers with whom you have no direct contacts	5.8	23.0	47.1	24.1	100.0
Your own staff arising from travel in foreign countries	58.6	23.0	10.3	8.1	100.0

Your own staff based on foreign magazines, newspapers, and so on	11.5	51.7	21.8	15.0	100.0
From your production staff	17.2	36.8	26.4	19.6	100.0
Other Korean firms	4.6	34.5	44.8	16.1	100.0
Affiliates or foreign branches of your firm	19.5	24.1	37.9	18.5	100.0
Your representatives or branch offices in foreign countries	29.9	21.8	28.7	19.6	100.0
Your foreign parent company (if any)	3.5	1.2	49.4	45.9	100.0
Your domestic parent company (if any)	18.4	13.8	25.3	42.5	100.0
Other	3.5	1.2	9.2	86.1	100.0

Note: Seventy-two of these eighty-seven firms had domestic sales as well as exports.

A–48. In obtaining export contracts between the beginning of 1975 and the middle of 1976, how would you rate price, delivery time, and the terms of credit in order of importance?

Factor and sector	Number of firms replying	Percentage of firms replying				
		Very important	Important	Of minor importance	Unimportant or not applicable	Total
Price						
Traditional sector	40	100.0	0.0	0.0	0.0	100.0
Resource-based sector	11	90.9	9.1	0.0	0.0	100.0
Modern sector	35	94.3	5.7	0.0	0.0	100.0
Trading companies	6	83.3	16.7	0.0	0.0	100.0
All sectors	92	95.7	4.3	0.0	0.0	100.0

Delivery time

Traditional sector	39	23.1	43.6	23.1	10.3	100.0
Resource-based sector	11	45.5	45.5	9.1	0.0	100.0
Modern sector	35	28.6	37.1	20.0	14.3	100.0
Trading companies	7	14.3	71.4	14.3	0.0	100.0
All sectors	92	27.2	43.5	19.6	9.8	100.0

Credit terms

Traditional sector	38	21.1	47.4	26.3	5.3	100.0
Resource-based sector	11	36.4	27.3	36.4	0.0	100.0
Modern sector	34	29.4	38.2	17.6	14.7	100.0
Trading companies	7	42.9	28.6	28.6	0.0	100.0
All sectors	90	27.8	40.0	24.4	7.8	100.0

A-49. During 1974–76 have you entered any export markets in which you expect to become important?

Yes 69   No 25   No reply 1

If, yes, please indicate the country or region and how the first contact was made:

										Central and South America	All new markets		Firms not specifying particular markets	
	Japan	Other Asia	U.S. and Canada	Middle East	Africa	Oceania	EEC	Other Europe		Number	Percent	Number	Percent
Number of firms that developed new markets	8	23	14	39	6	8	17	10	8	44	—	25	25
Source of initial contact not specified	1	2	2	5	—	1	2	—	2	—	—	—	—
Initial contact from:													
Buyers in foreign countries	5	10	8	7	2	4	7	2	—	45	28	16	25
Discussion following trade fairs	1	1	3	1	1	—	3	1	—	11	7	7	11
Foreign buyers visiting Korea	3	2	4	6	—	2	6	2	—	25	16	12	19
Inquiries from Korean trading firms	—	4	—	1	1	1	1	1	1	10	6	3	5

134

Other Korean firms already doing business in the foreign country	—	1	4	—	—	—	1	—	—	6	4	3	5
An enquiry directed to you through KOTRA	—	—	1	—	1	2	2	1	2	7	4	5	8
An enquiry directed to you through your trade association	—	2	—	—	—	—	—	1	—	4	3	—	—
An enquiry from a branch or affiliate of a foreign firm to which you were already exporting	1	3	1	5	1	1	1	2	—	14	9	7	11
A visit by a member of your own staff, or by your representatives to the country	1	6	4	15	1	1	2	1	3	34	21	9	14
Other means	—	2	1	1	—	1	—	1	—	6	4	2	3
Total	11	30	23	41	6	10	22	12	7	162	100	64	100

— Zero or not available.

Note: Forty-four firms distinguished their new export markets, but a few of these did not indicate how the first contact was made in some of the markets. The last column relates to twenty-five firms that indicated how their first contacts were made in different markets, but did not specify the markets.

A–50. *Please check which of the statements about changes in product lines and quality most accurately describe the development of your firm's manufacturing since 1971.*

	Export markets		Domestic market	
Change	*Number of firms*	*Percentage*	*Number of firms*	*Percentage*
Number of basic products				
Reduced	2	2.2	1	1.8
Kept about the same	19	21.3	17	30.4
Increased	68	76.4	38	67.9
Number of firms replying	89	100.0	56	100.0
Number of varieties of basic products				
Reduced	1	1.1	0	0.0
Kept about the same	26	29.5	20	36.4
Increased	61	69.3	35	63.6
Number of firms replying	88	100.0	55	100.0
General quality				
Reduced	0	0.0	0	0.0
Maintained about the same	7	8.0	7	12.5
Upgraded	79	89.8	49	87.5
No clear trend	2	2.3	0	0.0
Number of firms replying	88	100.0	56	100.0

Appendix B

Basic Economic Data

LIST OF TABLES

B-1. *Principal Economic Indicators, 1962–81*

	Percentage share in GNP					Average annual growth rate (percentage)[a]					
	1962	1967	1972	1977	1981	1962–67	1967–72	1972–77	1977–81	1977–79	1962–81
GNP[b]	100.0	100.0	100.0	100.0	100.0	8.7	9.5	11.0	4.3	9.0	8.6
Agriculture, forestry, and fishing	43.3	30.6	27.8	22.2	18.3	5.7	3.2	6.2	–0.6	1.2	3.8
Mining and manufacturing	11.1	21.0	22.3	30.6	35.9	15.7	18.5	18.3	8.6	14.6	15.5
Services	45.6	48.4	49.9	47.2	45.8	9.6	10.7	9.6	3.5	8.7	8.6
Consumption	100.5	89.0	86.9	74.7	77.2	6.2	9.0	7.7	5.2	9.2	7.1
Gross investment	9.6	21.9	24.2	31.0	33.2	26.1	13.6	16.7	6.1	26.4	15.9
Exports of goods and services	3.9	11.6	21.2	39.8	48.9	28.2	30.2	25.9	9.9	6.4	24.0
Imports of goods and services	13.8	22.5	30.6	45.6	54.1	17.2	19.2	20.3	8.9	18.4	16.7
Foreign saving[c]	10.7	8.8	5.3	0.6	7.9	—	—	—	—	—	—
Domestic saving[c]	3.3	11.4	15.7	25.1	19.6	—	—	—	—	—	—

Commodity exports[c]	2.4	7.4	15.8	28.6	34.2	42.3	38.4	44.0	20.6	22.4	36.9
Commodity imports[c]	18.2	23.3	24.6	30.7	42.0	18.8	20.4	33.8	24.7	37.2	24.3
Wholesale prices						15.6	9.3	18.6	22.6	15.2	15.3
Consumer prices						20.4	12.9	15.4	21.1	16.3	14.6

Millions of people

Population	26.6	30.1	32.7	36.4	38.7	2.4	1.9	1.9	1.6	1.6	2.0

U.S. dollars

GNP per capita[c]	87	142	306	966	1,607	10.3	16.6	25.9	13.6	26.5	16.6

— Zero or not available.

Note: Figures for 1981 are preliminary.

a. Calculated as a compound rate.

b. In 1975 market prices.

c. In current prices.

Sources: Population and GNP per capita from Bank of Korea, *National Income in Korea 1982*, and various issues of World Bank, *World Bank Atlas*; all others computed from data in various issues of Bank of Korea, *Economic Statistics Yearbook and Monthly Statistical Bulletin*.

B-2. Exports by Commodity Group and Major Commodity, 1962–81

Commodities	SITC code	1962	1967	1972	1977	1981	Average annual growth rate (percent)[a] 1962-67	1967-72	1972-77	1977-81
Total		100.0	100.0	100.0	100.0	100.0	42.3	38.4	44.0	20.6
Value (millions of current dollars)		54.8	320.2	1,624.1	10,046.5	21,253.8				
Percentage composition										
Primary products	0+1+2+3+4+68	80.5	33.3	16.3	15.0	9.5	19.3	19.9	31.9	7.5
Manufacturing sector	5+6+7+8+9−68	19.5	66.7	83.7	85.0	90.5	82.3	44.8	44.4	22.5
Chemicals	5	1.8	0.7	2.2	2.2	3.2	19.1	72.0	44.3	31.8
Manufactured goods classified by material	6	11.3	31.6	31.7	30.1	33.9	74.9	38.4	42.5	24.3
Rubber tires and tubes	6291	—	0.5	0.6	1.5	2.2	—	38.0	71.4	32.7
Wood and cork	63	4.2	11.4	10.5	4.2	2.1	73.9	36.0	20.0	1.0
Plywood	631211/16	0.7	11.4	9.5	3.2	1.5	78.3	33.7	15.7	0.3

Textiles	65	3.3	15.3	10.9	10.8	11.5	93.6	29.2	43.7	22.7
Cement	6612	—	0.0	0.8	1.5	1.6	—	—	64.2	21.6
Iron and steel	67	0.9	0.6	5.7	3.9	8.7	30.6	117.7	33.4	47.2
Nonferrous metals	68	—	0.6	0.4	0.3	0.5	—	26.8	40.7	36.4
Manufactures of metals	69	—	2.2	1.4	5.7	5.1	—	25.9	91.5	17.4
Machinery and transport equipment	7	2.6	4.4	10.6	17.3	22.2	58.9	64.6	59.0	28.3
Nonelectrical machinery	71	—	1.2	2.0	1.4	2.3	—	51.8	35.1	35.4
Electrical machinery and electronics	72	—	0.9	7.7	9.2	10.2	—	76.1	49.2	23.7
Transport equipment	73	—	0.8	0.9	6.7	9.7	—	38.6	116.1	32.2
Ships and boats	7353/9	—	—	0.0	5.2	6.6	—	—	287.8	28.0
Miscellaneous manufactured articles	8	3.6	30.4	39.6	35.3	31.2	117.4	46.0	40.7	17.0
Clothing	84	—	18.5	27.2	20.5	18.2	—	49.5	36.1	17.0
Footwear	85	—	2.5	3.4	4.9	4.8	—	46.9	54.5	20.4
Wigs	89995	—	7.1	4.5	0.6	0.2	—	26.6	-4.5	-2.5
Unclassified	9	0.2	0.0	0.0	0.4	0.5	14.9	28.5	25.6	27.2

— Zero or not available.

a. Calculated as a compound rate.

Source: Various issues of Bank of Korea, Economic Statistics Yearbook, and Monthly Statistical Bulletin.

B-3. *Annual Change in Principal Economic Indicators, 1976–82*

Indicator	Percentage change over preceding year						
	1976	1977	1978	1979	1980	1981	1982
Gross national product	15.1	10.3	11.6	6.4	−6.2	6.4	5.4
Manufacturing and mining	21.5	14.3	20.0	9.4	−1.1	7.2	3.7
Gross investment	8.0	24.0	35.9	17.5	−24.4	5.0	0.1
Exports of goods and services	43.0	25.7	17.5	−3.6	9.9	17.2	4.6
Imports of goods and services	26.9	23.8	29.1	8.6	−7.7	8.5	0.1
Wholesale prices	12.2	9.0	11.6	18.8	38.9	20.4	4.7
Consumer prices	15.3	10.2	14.5	18.3	28.7	21.3	7.3

Note: All percentages were calculated from data in 1975 market prices; those for 1982 are preliminary.
Sources: Computed from data in various issues of Bank of Korea, *Economic Statistics Yearbook* and *Monthly Statistical Bulletin.*

B-4. Exports by Destination, 1962–81

Destination	Millions of current dollars					Percentage composition				
	1962	1967	1972	1977	1981	1962	1967	1972	1977	1981
Total	54.8	320.2	1,624.1	10,046.5	21,253.8	100.0	100.0	100.0	100.0	100.0
Asia	35.7	129.1	591.2	4,250.5	8,325.0	65.1	40.3	36.4	42.3	39.2
Japan	23.5	84.7	407.9	2,148.3	3,502.8	42.9	26.5	25.1	21.3	16.5
Middle East a	0.1	1.2	10.8	1,040.6	1,344.6	0.2	0.4	0.7	10.4	6.3
Others	12.1	43.2	172.5	1,061.6	3,477.6	22.0	13.4	10.6	11.6	16.4
Europe	6.3	33.2	164.8	1,759.9	3,381.6	11.5	10.4	10.1	17.5	15.9
EEC b	5.9	23.6	115.3	1,397.5	2,612.5	10.8	7.4	7.1	13.9	12.3
Others	0.4	9.6	49.5	362.4	769.1	0.7	3.0	3.0	3.6	3.6
North America	12.1	146.0	827.1	3,535.6	6,477.8	22.1	45.6	50.9	35.2	30.5
United States	12.0	137.4	759.0	3,118.6	5,660.6	21.9	42.9	46.7	31.0	26.6
Canada	0.1	7.9	58.9	298.8	483.5	0.2	2.5	3.6	3.0	2.3
Others	—	0.7	9.2	118.2	333.7	—	0.2	0.6	1.2	1.6
South America	0.4	0.7	4.0	59.5	473.5	0.7	0.2	0.2	0.6	2.2
Africa	—	8.8	19.9	291.0	1,286.6	—	2.7	1.2	2.9	6.1
Oceania	0.2	3.0	15.0	142.6	365.7	0.4	0.9	0.9	1.4	1.7
Unclassified	1.0	0.0	2.1	8.3	943.5	1.8	—	0.1	0.0	4.4

— Zero or not available.
a. Includes Iran, Kuwait, and Saudi Arabia.
b. Excludes Ireland and Luxembourg.
Source: Various issues of Bank of Korea, Economic Statistics Yearbook.

143

B–5. *Export Targets and Performance, Korea, 1962–81*

Year	Millions of dollars				Percentage	
	Target in five-year plan	Initial target[a]	Final target[b]	Performance	Final target in relation to initial target	Performance in relation to final target
1962	60.9		61.9	56.7		92
1963	71.7		81.9	84.4		103
1964	84.1		120.0	120.9		101
1965	105.6		170.0	180.5		106
1966	117.5		250.0	255.8		102
1967	300.0	350	360.0	358.6	103	100
1968	360.0	450	500.0	500.0	111	100
1969	420.0	650	700.0	702.8	108	100
1970	480.0	936	1,000.0	1,003.8	107	100
1971	550.0	1,191	1,350.0	1,352.0	113	100

Year						
1972	1,680.0	1,435	1,800.0	1,807.0	125	100
1973	2,100.0	2,148	2,350.0	3,257.0	109	139
1974	2,521.0	4,468	4,500.0	4,712.9	101	105
1975	2,975.0	6,000	6,000.0	5,427.4	100	90
1976	3,510.0	6,500	6,500.0	7,715.1	100	119
1977	7,568.0	10,000	10,000.0	10,046.5	100	100
1978	8,892.0	12,500	12,500.0	12,710.6	100	102
1979	10,271.0	15,500	15,100.0	15,055.5	97	100
1980	11,657.0	17,000	17,000.0	17,505.0	100	103
1981	13,000.0	20,500	21,500.0	21,253.8	104	99

Note: Figures generally are in current prices and on the basis of cash receipts. The exceptions are the export figures for 1976–80, which are on the basis of customs clearance, and the Fourth Five-Year Plan targets, which are in 1975 prices.

a. Targets in the Overall Resource Budget (ORB) of the Economic Planning Board, which are the initial targets of the Ministry of Commerce and Industry.

b. Final targets of the Ministry of Commerce and Industry.

Sources: Exports for 1976–80 from Bank of Korea, *Monthly Economic Statistics,* February 1981; targets for 1977–81 from Korea Exchange Bank, *Monthly Review,* July 1976; initial ORB targets from the Ministry of Commerce and Industry; all others from Ministry of Commerce and Industry, *Trade Yearbook,* various years.

145

B-6. *Number of Overseas Offices of Korean Export Firms, by Region, 1968–79*

				Number of branches				
Year	Asia	Middle East	Europe	North America	Latin America	Oceania	Africa	Total
1968	93	0	4	92	0	2	3	194
1969	164	0	13	152	2	2	8	341
1970	139	5	23	155	10	5	10	347
1971	181	3	34	225	9	5	8	465
1972	186	5	43	220	12	10	9	485
1973	184	3	63	183	12	9	18	472
1974	261	25	76	200	16	7	15	600
1975	269	68	114	279	26	8	19	783
1976	273	102	163	392	41	14	17	1,002
1977	340	198	208	498	55	21	39	1,359
1978	384	231	209	510	60	26	42	1,462
1979 (June)	390	198	199	520	67	28	35	1,437[a]

a. Data for 1968–78 were based on approvals by the Ministry of Commerce and Industry; in 1979 about 180 inactive offices were eliminated from the roster.

B–7. *Branches of General Trading Companies, by Region and by Company, 1980*

		Number of branches						
Company	Asia	Middle East	Europe	North America	Latin America	Oceania	Africa	Total
Samsung	8	7	6	5	3	2	5	36
Ssangyong	6	7	1	3	2	2	2	23
Daewoo	10	5	6	8	3	1	6	39
Kukje	4	7	4	4	2	1	1	23
Hanil	7	3	4	4	0	1	1	20
Korea Trade	2	1	1	2	0	0	0	6
Hyo Sung	9	4	3	4	3	1	0	24
Bando	6	6	5	4	3	1	1	26
Sunkyong	5	4	5	15	4	0	2	35
Samwha	6	4	5	3	2	1	2	23
Kum Ho	3	5	7	3	2	1	1	22
Hyundai	8	12	8	8	5	1	3	45
Yulsan	7	14	1	4	3	1	2	32
Total	81	79	56	67	32	13	26	354

Source: Data supplied to the authors by the Korea International Economic Institute.

B-8. Exports of General Trading Companies, 1975–82

Company	Exports in millions of U.S. dollars								Average annual rate of increase, 1975–82 (percent)	Number of affiliated companies
	1975	1976	1977	1978	1979	1980	1981	1982		
Samsung	223	355	507	493	767	1,237	1,607	1,860	35.4	21
Ssangyong	125	141	176	265	420	642	756	972	34.0	14
Daewoo	161	301	501	709	1,119	1,415	1,914	1,971	43.0	26
Kukje	64	197	328	472	564	744	849	934	46.7	18
Hanil	37	218	127	188	—	—	—	—	—	—
Korea Trade[a]	—	18	25	24	51	67	84	75	26.9	—
Hyo Sung	—	113	199	338	583	764	787	599	32.0	23
Bando	—	134	212	330	467	493	619	689	31.4	22
Sunkyong	—	114	247	283	320	430	585	601	31.9	16

Samwha	—	—	167	260	—	—	—	—	—	—
Kum Ho	—	99	204	256	305	356	185	166	9.0	10
Hyundai	—	—	320	260	450	1,028	1,721	2,677	52.9	23
Yulsan	—	—	91	151	—	—	—	—	—	—
Total	610	1,690	3,104	4,029	5,046	7,176	9,107	10,544	50.2[b]	173
Percentage share of total in Korea's exports	12.0	21.9	30.9	31.7	33.5	41.0	42.8	48.2		

— Zero or data not available.

a. Korea Trade is an exporting agent for small and medium-scale producers.

b. The comparable rate for Korea's exports was 23.2 percent a year.

Source: Korean Traders Association, *The Structure of Korea's Exports and Import*, Seoul, September 1981, in Korean, except data for 1981 and 1982, for the number of affiliated companies, and for Hanil, Samwha, Yulsan, and Korea Trade, which are from the Korean daily, *Hankook Ilbo*, 25 June 1983.

B–9. *Investments and Domestic Bank Loans for the Machinery Industries, 1975–80*
(billions of Korean won; percent)

Item	1975	1976	1977	1978	1979	1980
Investments for manufacturing	627.2	827.9	1,379.3	2,148.1	2,685.6	—
Investments for machinery industries	123.0	178.9	278.1	545.5	886.9	—
Percentage share of investments for machinery industries in those for all manufacturing	19.6	21.4	20.2	25.4	33.0	—
Domestic bank loans for manufacturing	1,902.2	2,486.5	3,206.4	4,366.7	6,104.8	8,668.8
Domestic bank loans for machinery industries	358.4	504.8	762.7	1,099.5	1,653.5	2,599.9
Percentage share of bank loans for machinery industries in those for all manufacturing	18.8	20.3	23.8	25.2	27.1	30.0

— Zero data or not available.

Note: In the mid-1970s the exchange rate was 485 won to the U.S. dollar, in 1980, 580 won.

Source: Korea International Economic Institute (1980, p. 179) and Korea Development Institute (1982, Annex table 6).

References

The word "processed" describes works that are reproduced from typescript by mimeograph, xerography, or similar means. Such works are often not cataloged by or available through libraries, or may be subject to restricted circulation.

Arrow, Kenneth J. 1974a. "Limited Knowledge and Economic Analysis." *American Economic Review,* vol. 64, no. 1 (March), pp. 1–10.

———. 1974b. *The Limits of Organization.* New York: W. W. Norton.

Atkinson, Anthony B., and Joseph E. Stiglitz. 1969. "A New View of Technological Change." *The Economic Journal* (September), pp. 573–78.

Balassa, Bela. 1976. "Reforming the System of Incentives in Developing Countries." *World Development,* vol. 3, no. 6 (June 1976), pp. 365–82.

———. 1977. "Stages Approach to Comparative Advantage." A paper presented at the 5th World Congress of the International Economic Association.

———. 1983. "The Role of Foreign Trade in the Economic Development of Korea." Washington, D.C.: The World Bank. Processed.

Balassa, Bela, and Associates. 1971. *The Structure of Protection in Developing Countries.* Baltimore, Md.: Johns Hopkins University Press.

Balassa, Bela, and others. 1982. *Development Strategies in Semi-industrial Economies.* Baltimore, Md.: Johns Hopkins University Press.

Bell, Martin, Bruce Ross-Larson, and Larry Westphal. 1982. "The Cost and Benefit of Infant Industries: A Summary of Firm-Level Research." Paper presented at the 1982 Meeting of the American Economic Association. Washington, D.C.: The World Bank. Processed.

Bhagwati, Jagdish. 1978. *Anatomy and Consequences of Exchange Control Regimes.* Foreign Trade Regimes and Economic Development, vol. XI. New York: National Bureau of Economic Research.

Brash, Donald T. 1966. *American Investment in Australian Industry.* Canberra: Australian National University Press.

Bronte, Stephen. 1982. *Japanese Finance: Markets and Institutions*. London: Euromoney Publications.

Cole, David, and Yung Chul Park. 1983. *Financial Development in Korea: 1945–78*. Studies in the Modernization of the Republic of Korea. Cambridge, Mass.: Harvard University, Council on East Asian Studies.

Enos, John. 1982. "The Choice of Technique vs. the Choice of Beneficiary: What the Third World Chooses." In Frances Stewart and Jeffrey James (eds.), *The Economics of New Technology in Developing Countries*. London: Frances Pinter.

Frank, Charles R., Jr., Kim Kwang Suk, and Larry E. Westphal. 1975. *Foreign Trade Regimes and Economic Development: South Korea*. New York: National Bureau of Economic Research.

Hofheinz, Roy, Jr., and Kent E. Calder. 1982. *The East Asia Edge*. New York: Basic Books.

Hurwicz, Leonid. 1973. "The Design of Mechanisms for Resource Allocation." *American Economic Review*, vol. 63, no. 2 (May), pp. 1–30.

Institute of Economic Research, Seoul National University. 1979. "The Third Interim Report on 'The Absorption and Diffusion of Imported Technology in Korea.'" Seoul: Seoul National University. Processed.

Johnson, Chalmers. 1982. *MITI and the Japanese Miracle: The Growth of Industrial Policy, 1925–1975*. Stanford: Stanford University Press.

Jones, Leroy, P., and Il Sakong. 1980. *Government, Business, and Entrepreneurship in Economic Development: The Korean Case*. Studies in the Modernization of the Republic of Korea: 1945–1975. Cambridge, Mass.: Harvard University, Council on East Asian Studies.

Katz, Jorge. 1978. "Technological Change, Economic Development, and Intra and Extra Regional Relations in Latin America." Buenos Aires: IDB/ECLA Research Programme in Science and Technology, Working Paper, no. 3.

Keesing, Donald B. Forthcoming. *Exporting Manufactured Consumer Goods from Developing Countries*. Washington, D.C.: The World Bank.

Korea Development Institute. 1982. "Current Status and Major Issues of Korea's Industrial Incentives for the Mechanical Engineering Industries." Seoul. Processed in Korean.

Korea Economic Planning Board. 1982a. *Annual Economic White Paper, 1981*. In Korean. Seoul.

——. 1982b. *Economic Policies during Development Eras: Twenty-year History of the Economic Planning Board*. In Korean. Seoul.

Korea Economic Research Center. 1961. *Industrial Structure of Korea*, vol. 1: *Manufacturing Industries*. Seoul: Korean Traders Association and American-Korean Foundation.

Korea Federation of National Economic Associations. 1976. *Korean Economic Almanac.* Seoul.

——. 1982. *Private Sector Economic White Paper for 1982.* Seoul.

Korea International Economic Institute. 1980. *Current Status and Major Issues of Korea's Mechanical Engineering Industries.* In Korean. Seoul.

Korea Ministry of Commerce and Industry. 1974. *Annual Report, 1974.* In Korean. Seoul.

Korea Ministry of Science and Technology. 1977. *Science and Technology Annual, 1977.* Seoul.

Krueger, Anne O. 1978. *Foreign Trade Regimes and Economic Development: Liberalization Attempts and Consequences.* New York: Columbia University Press for the National Bureau of Economic Research.

——. 1980. *The Development Role of the Foreign Sector and Aid.* Studies in the Modernization of the Republic of Korea: 1945–1975. Cambridge, Mass.: Harvard University, Council on East Asian Studies.

——. 1981. "Export-led Industrial Growth Reconsidered." In Wontack Hong and Lawrence B. Krause (eds.), *Trade and Growth of the Advanced Developing Countries of the Pacific Basin.* Proceedings of the 11th Pacific Trade and Development Conference. Seoul: Korea Development Institute.

Lewis, Arthur. 1977. "The Less Developed Countries and Stable Exchange Rates." In *The International Monetary System in Operation.* The 1977 Per Jacobsson Lecture. Washington, D.C.: Per Jacobsson Foundation.

Little, I., T. Scitovsky, and M. Scott. 1970. *Industry and Trade in Some Developing Countries: A Comparative Study.* London: Oxford University Press for the Organisation for Economic Co-operation and Development.

Magaziner, Ira C., and Thomas M. Hout. 1980. *Japanese Industrial Policy.* Policy Papers in International Affairs, no. 15. Berkeley, Calif.: University of California, Institute of International Studies.

Mason, Edward S., and colleagues. 1980. *The Economic and Social Modernization of the Republic of Korea.* Studies in the Modernization of the Republic of Korea: 1945–1975. Cambridge, Mass.: Harvard University, Council on East Asian Studies.

Masubuchi, Koichi. 1981. "Technological Development in the Shipbuilding Industry in Korea." Cambridge and Seoul: Massachusetts Institute of Technology, Center for Policy Alternatives, and Korea Institute of Science and Technology. Processed.

McKinnon, Ronald. 1971. "On Misunderstanding the Capital Constraint in LDCs: the Consequences from Trade Policy." In Jagdish Bhagwati, Ronald Jones, Robert Mundell, and Jaroslav Vanek (eds.) *Trade, Balance of Payments and Growth: Papers in International Economics in Honour of Charles Kindleberger.* New York: North Holland.

———. 1979. "Foreign Trade Regimes and Economic Development: A Review Article." *Journal of International Economics*, vol. 9, pp. 429–52.

———. 1981. "Monetary Control and the Crawling Peg," in John Williamson (ed.), *Exchange Rate Rules.* New York: Macmillan.

Peck, Merton J. 1976. "Technology." In Hugh Patrick and Henry Rosovsky (eds.), *Asia's New Giant: How the Japanese Economy Works.* Washington, D.C.: Brookings Institution.

Rhee, Yung Whee. 1980. *An Investigation of the Economic Impact of Korea's Import Tariff Drawback System.* In Korean. Seoul: Korea International Economic Institute.

———. 1984. "Export Policy and Administration in Developing Economies." Washington, D.C.: The World Bank. Processed.

Rhee, Yung Whee, and Larry E. Westphal. 1977. "A Micro, Econometric Investigation of Choice of Technology." *Journal of Development Economics,* vol. 4, pp. 205–37.

Rhee, Yung Whee, and Young-Sun Lee. 1980. *Korean Export Marketing of Heavy Industrial Products: Status and Policy Direction.* In Korean. Seoul: Korea International Economic Institute.

Shinohara, Miyohei. 1982. "Japanese Experience in Managing Development." Background Paper for *World Development Report 1983.* Washington, D.C.: The World Bank. Processed.

Suh, Suk Tai. 1981. "The Effects of Export Incentives on Korean Export Growth: 1953–79." Korea Development Institute Working Paper 8107. Seoul: Korea Development Institute.

Vogel, Ezra F. 1979. *Japan as Number 1: Lessons for America.* Cambridge: Harvard University Press.

Westphal, Larry E. 1978. "The Republic of Korea's Experience with Export-led Industrial Development." *World Development,* vol. 6, no. 3, pp. 347–82.

———. 1981. "Empirical Justification for Infant Industry Protection." World Bank Staff Working Paper, no. 445. Washington, D.C.: The World Bank.

———. 1982a. "The Private Sector as 'Principal Engine' of Development: Korea." *Finance and Development,* vol. 19, no. 2, pp. 34–38.

———. 1982b. "Fostering Technological Mastery by Means of Selective Infant-Industry Protection." In Moshe Syrquin and Simon Teitel (eds.), *Trade, Stability, Technology and Equity in Latin America.* New York: Academic Press.

Westphal, Larry, and Irma Adelman. 1973. "Reflections on the Political Economy of Planning: The Case of Korea." *Journal of East-West Studies* (Yonsei University, Seoul). October, pp. 95–116.

Westphal, Larry E., and Kwang Suk Kim. 1977. "Industrial Policy and Development in Korea." World Bank Staff Working Paper, no. 263. Washington, D.C.: The World Bank.

Westphal, Larry E., Yung Whee Rhee, Linsu Kim, and Alice Amsden. 1984. "Exports of Capital Goods and Related Services from the Republic of Korea." World Bank Staff Working Paper, no. 629. Washington, D.C.: The World Bank.

Westphal, Larry E., Yung Whee Rhee, and Garry Pursell (1981). "Korean Industrial Competence: Where It Came From." World Bank Staff Working Paper, no. 469. Washington, D.C.: The World Bank, 1981.

Wortzel, Lawrence H., and Heidi V. Wortzel. 1980. "Indigenous Manufacturing Firms from LDCs and NICs as Export Marketers: Progress and Strategic Recommendations." Washington, D.C.: The World Bank. Processed.

Young, Alexander K. 1979. *The Sogo Shosha: Japan's Multinational Trading Companies.* Boulder, Colo.: Westview.

Index

Advertising, in foreign markets, 51, 55, 56, 63
Apparel. *See* Clothing industry
Appliances, buyer influence on design of, 63
Atkinson, Anthony B., 42
Automobile industry: buyer influence on, 62–63; overseas branches of, 65n
Awards for achievement, 17–18, 31, 37

Balance of payments, 9, 36
Balassa, Bela, 3, 44, 68
Bank of Korea, 12, 14
Banks: commercial, 6,10, 11, 12–13, 14; export financing and, 6, 9–10, 11, 12–13, 14–15, 16, 28, 72; private control of Japanese, 6; government control of Korean, 6, 11, 13–15, 28
Branches: of foreign firms in Korea, 56; of Korean firms abroad, 53–54, 65n, 72; of Korean firms as foreign buyers, 57, 59
Brand names, use of, 63, 64
Brash, Donald T., 42
Brazil, steel industry in, 48
Bundled and unbundled imported technological packages, 44, 45–56, 71
Bureaucracy: bypassing of, 69–70; efficiency of, 5, 12–13, 15, 16, 30–31, 35–36, 73
Business-government alliance, 5–6, 12–13, 15–18, 21–38; breakdown of, 67, 69–70; needs for 1980s and, 70–71

Buyers, foreign: as technology sources, 41–49; courting of, 52–56, 64–65, 65n–66n; ranked by size and industry, 51, 57–61; maintaining relations with, 55–56; marketing tasks performed by, 51, 61–64

Calder, Kent E., 6
Canada: branches and affiliates in, 54; Korean market in, 55
Capability, accumulation of technological, 44–49, 49n, 69, 71
Capital: investment, 13, 14–15, 68; loans for, 10, 11, 12, 14–15; resources, 6, 9–10, 11, 12, 13–15
Carter, Jimmy, and U.S. troop withdrawal, 67–68
Cement industry: brand name use by, 64; buyer influence on, 63; overseas branches of, 65n; technology sources for, 43, 44
Chemicals industry, technology sources for, 46
China, 31
Clothing industry: brand name use by, 64; foreign markets and, 59, 61; sales force abroad and, 63; technology sources for, 46
Communication, international, 51
Competition, in world markets, 3, 7, 15, 37; among firm heads, 17, 24–27, 34–37, 69–70; by heavy industry, 36, 67–70; by other developing countries, 72–75; for imported intermediate

The full range of World Bank publications, both free and for sale, is described in the *Catalog of Publications*; the continuing research program is outlined in *Abstracts of Current Studies*. Both booklets are updated annually; the most recent edition of each is available without charge from the Publications Distribution Unit, Department B, The World Bank, 1818 H Street, N.W., Washington, D.C. 20433, U.S.A.

Yung Whee Rhee is a senior economist in the Industry Department, Bruce Ross-Larson is a consultant, and Garry Pursell is an economist in the Industry Department, all at the World Bank.